THE DOG'S GUIDE TO YOUR
HAPPINESS

Garry McDaniel & Sharon Massen

lumina
MEDIA

Project Team

Editor: Amy Deputato
Copy Editor: Joann Woy
Design: Mary Ann Kahn
Index: Elizabeth Walker

LUMINA MEDIA™

Chairman: David Fry
Chief Executive Officer: Keith Walter
Chief Financial Officer: David Katzoff
Chief Digital Officer: Jennifer Black-Glover
Senior Vice President, Retail: Scott Coffman
Vice President Content: Joyce Bautista-Ferrari
Vice President Marketing & PR: Cameron
    Triebwasser
Managing Director, Books: Christopher
    Reggio
Art Director, Books: Mary Ann Kahn
Senior Editor, Books: Amy Deputato
Production Director: Laurie Panaggio
Production Manager: Jessica Jaensch

Library of Congress Cataloging-in-Publication Data
Names: McDaniel, Garry L., author. | Massen, Sharon, author.
Title: The dog's guide to your happiness : seven secrets for a better life
    from man's best friend / Garry McDaniel and Sharon Massen.
Description: Irvine, CA : Lumina Media, 2017. | Includes index.
Identifiers: LCCN 2016047298 | ISBN 9781621871682 (softcover)
Subjects: LCSH: Dogs--Behavior. | Dogs--Psychology. | Social values. |
    Happiness.
Classification: LCC SF433 .M344 2017 | DDC 636.7--dc23
LC record available at https://lccn.loc.gov/2016047298

2030 Main Street, Suite 1400
Irvine, CA 92614
www.facebook.com/luminamediabooks
www.luminamedia.com

Printed and bound in China
20 19 18 17   2 4 6 8 10 9 7 5 3 1

CONTENTS

PREFACE

The dog represents all that is best in man.

—Etienne Charlet

The purpose of this book is to give you enjoyment as well as encouragement to share the life and love of a dog. Dogs have long been known as mankind's best friend; we intend to demonstrate this by sharing not only documented research studies and other information found by professionals in the field of dog behavior and psychology and the stories of many dog owners—stories that illustrate not only the dogs' deep love for and devotion to their human companions but also their affection for other animal companions.

This book is designed to give you an appreciation of the ways in which dogs can guide us to experience greater happiness. Loyalty, communication, play, unconditional love, forgiveness, positive attitude, and life balance. Each chapter provides activities and questions to help you, the reader, take ownership of the concepts and attributes being fostered through the companionship of your dog. We believe that this book can help all who read it become better people—better workers, managers, parents, children—and better human companions of those animals who love them and display the seven secrets to happiness every day.

Read and enjoy! We would love to hear from you and share your stories.

INTRODUCTION

*I*n January 2016, tens of millions of Americans bought lottery tickets for the opportunity to win more than $1.5 billion dollars.[1] During the week leading to the selection of the winning numbers, crews from major networks fanned out across the country to ask the people standing in lines, waiting to buy lottery tickets, what they would do with the money if they won. Most said they would quit their jobs and use the money to buy an expensive car or mansion, travel the world, go back to college, or pay off all of their relatives' bills. Many of these individuals, like most people, assumed that buying more things would bring them greater happiness and joy in life. In this book, you will learn that happiness in life comes not from acquiring more "stuff" but from emulating seven secrets that mankind's best friend, the dog, models for us every day.

HAPPY DOG, HAPPY LIFE

Happiness is an aspiration that people have sought throughout the ages. Thousands of years ago, early Greek philosophers actually had a term, eudemonia, to describe happiness as the highest level of human good.[2] In the United States, our founding fathers included the values of "life, liberty and the pursuit of happiness"[3] in the Declaration of Independence as an inalienable right bestowed upon us by our Creator. But "happiness" means different things to different people. Fortunately, there has been considerable research into what comprises and defines a happy life. Psychologist and former Harvard Business School lecturer, Tal Ben-Sharar, describes a happy life as one in which a person, "enjoys positive emotions while perceiving [his or her] life as purposeful."[4] Professor Ben-Sharar emphasizes that this does not mean every moment of a happy life is nirvana. Rather, he means that even those living what they consider happy lives experience high and low points. The difference is that the happiest people choose to view and experience life from an overall positive perspective. So what does this have to do with dogs?

---

1   Retrieved from http://money.cnn.com/2016/01/13/news/powerball-drawing-tonight/

2   Retrieved from http://www.philosophybasics.com/branch_eudaimonism.html

3   Declaration of Independence, July 4, 1776.

4   Ben-Sharar, T. (2002). *The Question of Happiness: On Finding Meaning, Pleasure and the Ultimate Currency.* Lincoln, NE: Writers Club Press, p. 18.

Both of us have had dogs all our lives, and it is our observation that dogs are probably the most genuinely happy animals in the world. Some pets, such as goldfish, turtles, hamsters, and parakeets, give little to no indication as to how happy they are, while others—cats for example—are a bit easier to read. We are also aware that some animals, like the bottlenose porpoise, look happy, but perhaps this is because they have perpetual smiles. Dogs, on the other hand, give very clear feedback as to how much they are enjoying the world around them; from our perspective, unless they are being abused, they are very happy almost all the time. You can just tell that a dog is having the time of his life when he opens his mouth, lolls his tongue out, and grins. Sometimes we just sit back, watch dogs, and wonder what makes them so incomparably happy.

Garry has an English Springer Spaniel named Panda who seems unabashedly happy whether he is going for a walk, sniffing a tree, chasing a leaf, greeting a visitor, playing with a new toy, sitting in Garry's lap, jumping down from his lap, or tasting anything that drops on the floor. Ninety-nine percent of the time, Panda has the same happy smile on his face, and his little stub of a tail is wagging. Of course, there is also the other 1 percent of the time when Panda is clearly not happy. For example, Panda is not particularly fond of the vacuum cleaner, getting a bath, or having his nails trimmed. That said, Garry will tell you that Panda is very happy when the vacuum cleaner is turned off, when he jumps out of the tub, and the second the perpetrator stops trimming his toenails. So, while he is not happy every minute of the day, Panda and almost every other dog we have known appear genuinely predisposed to being happy. Can you say that about yourself and most of the people you know?

We do acknowledge that some dogs are in abusive settings and are clearly not happy with their circumstances or how they are treated. Yet it is remarkable to note that when these dogs are rescued from horrendous conditions and placed with loving families, they often quickly learn to love and trust, and they begin to live happier lives. Garry's family experienced this firsthand when they rescued a Miniature Dachshund named Princess. Because Princess cowered and shivered every time a family member picked up a magazine or newspaper to read, they surmised that her previous owner must have beat her regularly with one or both of these items. Yet, after months of patient care and support, Princess learned to accept that she was now part of a family who loved her and would not abuse her

in any way. Princess was able to transition from spending her time quivering in fear to exuberantly running, playing, and interacting with each of her new family members. With the right care and attention, Princess was able to evolve from living a life of constant terror to one where her joy and trust were evident.

Sharon remembers one of her treasured dogs who came to live with her family when she was seven years old. Snowdie was a small Rat Terrier whose previous humans felt she no longer fit into their happy home and asked Sharon's dad if he wanted to take her in. Knowing how much the family loved their Gladys, who had recently been killed by a reckless driver running up on the side of the road, he immediately said yes.

That Saturday morning, the owners brought over Snowdie, who got out of the car, walked directly into the house as if she had always lived there, and disappeared. Sharon's family said good-bye to the previous owners and began to search the house for Snowdie. They looked in the kitchen and the living room, but no Snowdie. Sharon then went to her bedroom, and there was Snowdie. She had climbed up on the bed and somehow pulled the covers up to her head and was comfortably situated on the pillow. And that became her spot, where she and Sharon shared tears, laughs, love, and secrets for many years.

Some argue that dogs are happier than humans because they lead such simple lives, with few demands and responsibilities. We agree. Human beings certainly have much more complex and stressful lives than dogs. In fact, we believe that our hectic, frenzied pace of life today actually works against our taking time to focus upon and appreciate what might contribute to more happiness in our lives. As Jim Loehr and Tony Schwartz observe in their book, *The Power of Full Engagement* (Free Press, 2003), "We use words like obsessed, crazed, and overwhelmed not to describe insanity, but instead to characterize our everyday lives. Feeling forever starved for time, we assume that we have no choice but to cram as much as possible in every day."

In our hearts, we know that cramming more and more into each day will not bring us the quality of relationship or the sense of happiness we desire, but we're so accustomed to living under constant demands that we don't know how to get off the treadmill and focus on what we know is central to a more stress-free and vibrant life filled with more meaningful relationships.

So, yes, dogs do have much simpler lives than human beings, but this does not mean that we can't learn from them or that we are absolved from taking control of and improving our lives and theirs. Dogs react to their circumstances primarily through heredity and instinct. Human beings, on the other hand, have the ability to rise above gut-level responses to what happens to us and choose how we will respond to our circumstances. What makes human beings so different from any other animal is our amazing ability to learn from the past, critically evaluate our current situation, envision a better future, and take action to create that future. We don't have to be passive pawns to the trials and tribulations life throws our way. We can choose to create a happy life. Fortunately, we have a great model that can help us evaluate and act upon the secrets that contribute to a greater level of joy, health, and life balance. That model, of course, is the dog.

WHY DO WE ADMIRE DOGS?

Human beings have had a unique and wonderful relationship with dogs for tens of thousands of years. In developing this book, both of us read extensively and spoke to experts, colleagues, and friends to understand why humans have had such a long-term close relationship with dogs. Moreover, we also wanted to understand why we perceive dogs as being such happy creatures and why the mere presence of a dog encourages many of us to be happier in our own lives. What was discovered is that (1) there are many qualities we admire in dogs that exemplify a happy life, and (2) these qualities complement each other to enhance an individual's level of happiness even more than any one quality can on its own. Let's look at these two points one at a time.

First, while there are dozens of qualities that could exemplify a happy life, seven "secrets" were consistently identified as those we most admire in our canine companions and that contribute to a dog's happy life. Interestingly, these seven secrets are also evident in the lives of humans. We believe that if we integrated these seven secrets routinely into our own lives, we would lead happier lives, too. The seven secrets of happiness, which will be discussed in greater detail in later chapters, are:

Loyalty: The willingness to make an appropriate investment or personal sacrifice to strengthen or sustain friendships and relationships with others.

Communication: How to listen to others and how to convey your message in a way that maximizes the chance that it will be received and interpreted correctly. This includes understanding what factors contribute to effective communication.

Play: The willingness to step outside of the routine and experience activities that are primarily recreational and just fun.

Forgiveness: The willingness to let go of animosity, bitterness, and resentment toward oneself or others.

Unconditional love: Expecting nothing in return from others for giving your own love.

Positive attitude: Seeing the dog bowl as half full rather than as half empty.

Work-Life balance: Attaining proper prioritization between work (career and ambition) and lifestyle (health, pleasure, leisure, family, and spiritual development).

Second, while each of the seven secrets has its own distinct value, we believe that, when practiced collectively, they provide extraordinary power toward living a life that is even more vibrant, fulfilled, and happy. For example, we would all agree that it is beneficial to communicate effectively with others. We would also agree that relationships are strengthened and trust is enhanced when we demonstrate loyalty in an appropriate and consistent manner. However, if you could exhibit effective communication and loyalty together, the positive impact upon yourself and others would be magnified. Imagine what it would mean if you added positive levels of loyalty, communication, play, forgiveness, unconditional love, a positive attitude, and balance in your life! We like to visualize the synergistic effect of these secrets as interrelating to and building upon each other as shown in the overlapping circles in Figure I.

How would your life change for the better if you harbored fewer grudges against others, if you stepped out of your comfort zone and experienced more of life, if you loved others unconditionally, if you went through life with a more positive attitude? If you attained a greater sense of life balance, wouldn't your life be happier? Wouldn't you like to go through life with these seven secrets of happiness?

The good news is that you can. And while this book is not intended to cover all possible steps that one could take to be successful in life, our goal is to share

Figure 1

some observations on these seven qualities that we witness in dogs, which we also believe can serve as a model for how we can all live more effective, joyful, fulfilling, and happy lives. We will begin by sharing some background information to help you understand how our relationship with dogs has come to be. Next, we will discuss the seven secrets we admire about dogs by describing each characteristic individually, discussing why humans value that quality so much in dogs, and exploring how that quality relates to humans and enhances our own lives. At the end of each chapter, we will provide a few questions and/or activities designed to help you reflect upon your current level of happiness and the application of one or more of the seven qualities in your life.

We hope that what you discover about dogs and humans in the pages that follow will prompt you to reflect deeply on your own perspective and to consider how you can develop and incorporate these canine secrets of happiness into your daily routine. It's time to rediscover the magic in your life—through the eyes of humanity's best friend.

Thinking about Happiness

Taking control of your future. One of the biggest drivers of personal happiness is the belief that we have control over our own future and that the actions we take make a difference. With all of the demands on our lives in today's busy world, it is easy to become overwhelmed if we try to fix all of our problems at once. It makes better sense to try and solve one problem at a time.

"THREE GOOD THINGS" EXERCISE

Sometimes we tend to focus on what has gone wrong and forget that there are many positive aspects of our lives, too. In the first column below, write down three things that made you happy during the past month. These can be relatively minor in importance ("I went jogging" or "I got to see my best friend") or they can be huge ("I got a new job with a big salary increase!") Next, answer the questions that follow in the other columns.

WHAT MADE ME HAPPY?	WHY DID THIS HAPPY EVENT OCCUR?	WHY DOES THIS MAKE ME HAPPY?	HOW CAN I ENSURE THAT THIS HAPPY EVENT KEEPS OCCURRING?

PERSONAL REFLECTION EXERCISE

An important aspect of our happiness is the quality of our personal relationships with others. In this activity, take a few minutes to think about your relationships with dogs. What made the relationship so special? Why did this relationship make you happy? What does this tell you about how you might enhance the relationships you have not only with your dog but also with your family, friends, and colleagues?

WRITING EXERCISE

In the space below, identify one achievable aspect of your life, a relationship, or your job upon which you could act and that would make you happier this week. What can you do to focus your efforts on achieving this one desired outcome? How will you know if you are making progress?

CHAPTER 1
LOYALTY

*We long for affection
altogether ignorant
of our faults.
Heaven has accorded this
to us in the uncritical
canine attachment.*

—GEORGE ELIOT

*O*ne of the benefits of writing and speaking about dogs is that other dog lovers send a steady stream of articles, book references, and links to stories on the Web about dogs. A great many of these articles and stories relate to how much we appreciate the loyalty that dogs show toward humans. If you conduct a Google search on the term dog loyalty, you will get more than 28 million hits, covering everything from which breeds are most loyal to true stories of dogs' loyalty to cartoon drawing depicting loyal dogs. Sometimes, the loyalty of dogs is demonstrated in home videos of dogs who are wildly excited at the return of owners who have been serving overseas with the military for extended periods of time. Other videos and articles take a more somber tone and profile dogs who have stayed at the side of their deceased human or canine companions for hours, days, weeks... And, of course, there are many stories about dogs who have demonstrated their loyalty by rescuing individuals or entire families from dangerous situations, such as home fires or gas leaks, or protected their owners from poisonous snakes, burglars, or attacks by other animals.

CIVIL WAR DOG

We have found that when we speak with groups, it is not uncommon for individuals to approach us before or after a lecture to share stories. On one memorable occasion, a woman shared a link to the story of Sallie, a brindle Bull Terrier who served as the mascot for the 11th Pennsylvania Volunteer Infantry Regiment during the American Civil War.[1] Sallie was given to the captain of the regiment when she was only five weeks old. As you might guess, in a situation where training for war was the primary focus of the troops, Sallie provided a welcome distraction to both the captain and the soldiers. Having served his time in basic training, Garry can empathize with how much the soldiers would have enjoyed having a cute puppy to play with, hold, and feed during those trying times.

As we all know, dogs are keen observers of human behavior and easily learn our routines. It should come as no surprise that, as the regimental mascot, Sallie learned to recognize the drum roll for reveille and was always the first out of the tent to attend roll call with her natural puppy enthusiasm. During marching drills, she would latch on to a particular soldier and prance alongside him during the exercises. When the troops performed a dress parade, she would station herself beside the regimental flag. At night, she slept in the captain's tent after strolling through the camp on an inspection of her own.

The 11th Pennsylvania saw its first action at Cedar Mountain, in 1862, and Sallie remained with the regimental flag throughout the entire engagement. Other major engagements followed at Antietam, Fredericksburg, and Chancellorsville. At each, Sallie would race around the front line, barking ferociously at the enemy.

Occasionally, in between battles, a visiting dignitary would arrive, requiring the troops to march in a formal "pass and review." In the spring of 1863, Sallie was marching with the regiment past the reviewing stand, which included a tall man with a stovepipe hat. That distinguished guest was none other than Abraham Lincoln, who, with a twinkle in his eye, raised his hat in salute to the regiment's mascot.

On the first day of fighting at Gettysburg, the 11th Pennsylvania was one of the first units engaged with the Confederates and, after a fierce fight, was driven back from their position on Oak Ridge and into town. During the chaos, Sallie became lost. She was found three days later by a soldier from the 12th Massachusetts.

---

1   Retrieved May 15, 2015, from www.nycivilwar.us/sallie.html

Sallie had found her way back to the regiment's original position on Oak Ridge and was standing guard over the bodies of her dead compatriots. Even though she was both hungry and thirsty, Sallie had stayed with the fallen troops.

Following the battle of Gettysburg, Sallie continued to serve in fight after fight. On February 6, 1865, the 11th Pennsylvania made a resolute attack upon the rebel lines at Hatcher's Run. As always, Sallie was in the first line of attack. Men in the second wave were advancing under heavy fire when they came upon the body of Sallie, who had been shot and killed. While still under fire from Confederate forces, the men of the 11th Pennsylvania buried Sallie where she had fallen on the battlefield.

However, the story does not stop there. In 1890, the surviving members of the 11th Pennsylvania Volunteer Infantry dedicated a monument on the Gettysburg battlefield to all of the men who had fought and died during that great battle. If you enter the search terms "Sallie" and "Gettysburg," in your Internet browser, you should find the monument, which features a Union soldier looking out over the fields in the direction from which the rebels came. But, there is something else on the monument that many visitors do not see unless they get out of their cars and walk around to the front. The soldiers of the 11th Pennsylvania ensured that a bronze likeness of Sallie was included at the base of the monument. Sallie was so loyal that her soldiers insisted that she be remembered on their monument for all time.

WHY IS LOYALTY IMPORTANT?

When we share the story of Sallie with groups of people or show them videos of a dog wiggling and jumping in wild abandon at the return of a long-lost owner, these people are often visibly moved. This raises an important question: why does the story of Sallie and the soldiers touch us so? Why did battle-hardened soldiers who had seen and lived through all manner of death, illness, and horrible conditions insist on including a dog on their monument? Why does it touch our hearts to see a dog's unabashed joy at being reunited with his owner? For those of us who have a dog, why is it so pleasurable to return home and be greeted with such elation? Why is loyalty so important to us?

To answer this question, let's begin by simply looking at how the word "loyalty" is defined. Definitions from various sources use words such as "faithfulness," "devotion," and "attachment."[2] Garry posed this question to his wife, Lauren, and she replied, "That's simple. People like certainty in relationships. Being loyal means you know you can count on others to be true to you and do the right thing even if it is difficult and even if you are not physically present."

Note that her definition includes two very important elements. First, a critical part of loyalty is that you feel confident that another person will be true to you and do the right thing. Second, a loyal person will be true to you and do the right thing even when you are not present. If you think about someone you do not feel is loyal, we are willing to bet that a big part of the reason is that you have little confidence that he or she will represent you well and stand up for you when he or she should. Dogs, on the other hand, are consistently loyal to their loving family members no matter the situation. People offer a number of suggestions as to why dogs are so loyal.

---

2   Retrieved from http://dictionary.reference.com/browse/Loyalty

Some suggest dogs are loyal only because they depend on us for food and shelter. From this point of view, dogs are loyal only because they have to be. However, we need look no further than our canine companions to see that real loyalty is alive and well. In our dogs, we see daily and consistent examples of loyalty at its finest.

ROOTS IN THE WOLF FAMILY TREE

Loyalty in dogs traces back to their roots as wolves. Researchers have found that a wolf pack in the wild is generally comprised of a tight-knit social group of family members who are intensely loyal to each other. This is for good reason. While a single wolf can survive on its own, membership in and loyalty to a group provides great benefits.

First, being a member of a group provides a higher level of safety and security. Where one animal might be attacked by a predator, a pack provides extra eyes and ears to spot danger—and more teeth to provide defense in the event of attack. Second, belonging to a group provides the opportunity to share the workload. Members of wolf packs share duties such as hunting, caring for pups, and educating younger wolves in the nuances of stalking and hunting prey, and if one pack member is injured, other members will bring it food until it's able to fend for itself again. Third, being part of a family allows wolves to create strong inter-pack relationships with others and, at some point, to mate and raise families of their own. Finally, being a pack member allows an animal to achieve a certain level of status in the pack hierarchy and potentially rise to a responsible role during the hunt.[3]

Because dogs trace their heredity back to wolves, it's not surprising that domesticated dogs view their human counterparts as part of their "pack." Like wolves, there are examples of single dogs surviving on their own; however, most have thrived through their relationships with humans. For a dog, being a member of a human family provides a level of safety and security unheard of in the wild. Our pets live in homes that are heated and air conditioned, where food and water are plentiful, and where there is little chance they'll become prey for another animal. As members of our families, dogs are often doted on and given a great level of affection. Many owners consider their dogs to be part of the family, and losing a pet can be as agonizing as losing a human loved one.

Dogs appear to take their roles as family members quite seriously, and they seem to enjoy a level of purpose and achievement from playing their part. Sled dogs, for

European gray wolf

3   Interview with Dr. Suzanne Waller, Professor of Sociology, Franklin University, March 1, 2014.

instance, eagerly seek the opportunity to pull sleds hundreds of miles, and they act depressed if not allowed to do so. Hunting dogs enthusiastically join their masters to find game. Herding dogs, such as Border Collies, work together to herd sheep with great skill, focus, and enjoyment of being able to do what they do best. One can also remember the search-and-rescue dogs who worked in the aftermath of the September 11 attacks; they would become depressed when they went for hours without finding a trapped person.[4] Working alongside humans, dogs can realize their full potential by doing what they most enjoy.

The benefits are not one-sided, however; humans also gain much from our relationship with dogs. Thanks to their loyalty, we can count on our dogs to warn us of intruders and other dangers. We take pride in their willingness and ability to play with our children, protect our households, and simply keep us company as we read, watch TV, or do chores around the home. Dogs are true companions who often seem happiest just being with us.

For instance, Garry notes that at the time he was writing this section of the book, Panda was lying at his feet. Whenever Garry would get up to get a drink or something to eat, Panda would get up and follow along right behind him. At one point during the day, Garry had to shovel the snow off the driveway. Panda insisted on coming along and was absolutely delighted in chasing every shovelful of snow that Garry tossed. As Garry shoveled, neighbors came outside with their dogs, and Panda took the opportunity to socialize with each neighbor and dog.

Dogs relish having jobs to do for their humans.

---

4   Retrieved from http://healthypets.mercola.com/sites/healthypets/archive/2011/09/08/remembering-the-dog-heroes-of-september-11th.aspx

The dogs had a blast chasing each other through the snow—mouths open wide in big doggy grins and tongues hanging out of their mouths as they crashed through the snow and romped across yards. However, throughout the fun, Panda would stop periodically to ensure that he could still see Garry as he shoveled. Occasionally, Panda would dash back just to run a circle around Garry before running off to frolic with his friends some more. In doing so, Panda was demonstrating his loyalty to Garry by checking in from time to time and always making sure that he knew where Garry was and that Garry knew where he was.

Of course, our dogs' loyalty goes well beyond following wherever we go and keeping tabs on us. Our dogs are always there when anyone in the family is ill or feeling down. A dog seems to sense when someone isn't at his or her best and will often come and sit with that person and lay his head on his or her lap. When children are upset, the family dog is there to share their disappointment; when they are excited, the dog is happy to joyfully dance around with them.

LOYAL FRIENDS

Loyalty can also extend from one dog to another. The following true story happened to Darrell Upp of Greenfield, Ohio, as he took his two dogs outside around midnight one night to "go potty." Upp's property has a I-acre side yard, bordered on one side by woods and on the other three sides by corn and bean fields. Skeeter is a 13-pound, 9-year-old male Miniature Rat Terrier with a Napoleon complex, and Bella is a 75-pound, 3-year-old female Bulldog who rules the roost and considers Skeeter to be her own personal plaything.

As Upp stood on the back porch that night, he noticed Skeeter's head suddenly jerk toward the woods. Snarling and growling like the 200-pound Rottweiler he believes himself to be, he darted off into the darkness, only to be heard screaming in pain moments later. Bella instantly raced toward the noise. As Upp sprinted after her, he saw Skeeter being shaken by a coyote several yards away. Upp said, "Now, for those of you who believe the Bulldog to be a slow, overweight, lethargic breed, let me tell you that Bella covered the 40-yard distance in seconds and slammed into that coyote like a runaway freight train, knocking him to the ground and freeing Skeeter."

As Bella chased the stunned coyote into the woods, Upp picked up Skeeter and carried him into the house. Bella returned and lay on the floor beside Upp as he inspected and cleaned Skeeter's wounds. The wounds were quite severe, and Upp did not expect the little warrior to survive. Bella stayed beside Skeeter's crate all night and accompanied Upp and Skeeter to the vet's office the next morning.

Personal Activity 1:

LOYALTY

Think about what you have read so far in this chapter on loyalty. Can you relate to it? Has there been a time when you acted out of total regard for a person or a pet who you tried to save or did save from a tragedy? Or have you witnessed someone else going that extra mile to save another person or animal from sorrow or from serious harm? If so, jot those instances down so that you can refer to them again later.

_____

Notes:

After three days, Skeeter was doing much better, although still a bit traumatized, and Upp was happy to report that he made a full recovery. Although Bella has determined that Skeeter is well enough for her to resume her duties as the daily thorn in his side, Upp has observed her standing guard, surveying the area, and watching over him whenever the two of them go outside to play or relieve themselves.

Looking back on this crisis in the lives of these two animals, it is very evident that Bella acted in total disregard for her own life and safety, throwing caution aside to save her little buddy. It was a total act of self-sacrifice, with one of them willing to lay down her life for the other. Thank goodness that this story has a happy ending.

THE EROSION OF LOYALTY

Clearly, loyalty is valued by people the world over. Unfortunately, many feel loyalty is disappearing from our personal and business relationships as society becomes increasingly individualized. One of the factors leading to the erosion of loyalty is that we've shifted from a culture based on long-term loyalty to one in which short-term, superficial relationships are increasingly the norm. In the "good old days," families depended on each other when faced with hardships and counted on each other to share food, money, housing, and transportation. The family unit was the nucleus of life, and whether raising a barn, building a house, holding a dance, or watching each other's children, families banded together. The same could be said for close networks such as friends, neighbors, and community groups such as a person's church, temple, mosque, or synagogue.

In an interesting research study, sociology professor Donald Kraybill examined which groups in the United States report being happiest in life. And do you know which group rated itself highest in happiness? The Amish. As you may know, the Amish community places a high value on its sense of collective identity and displays an intense loyalty to one another. The roots of their loyalty are based firmly in doing what is important for the community and not just for themselves. This perspective is summed up by an Amish woman in the study who said, "You have lots of cousins, maybe 100 or 150, who will always be there to take care of you if you have a need."[5]

How many of us can say the same thing for the network of people we count on? We count ourselves blessed if we can name a handful of people whom we can count on in any situation, let alone 100 or 150.

So, if loyalty is such a good thing, why does it appear to be becoming rarer in our society? One answer is that as individuals

---

5   Keiningham, T. & Aksoy, L. (2010). *Why Loyalty Matters: The Groundbreaking Approach to Rediscovering Happiness, Meaning and Lasting Fulfillment in Your Life and Work*, Dallas, TX: BenBella Books, p. 19.

we have become more mobile and less tied down by the things that used to bind us together. In their insightful book, Why Loyalty Matters: The Groundbreaking Approach to Rediscovering Happiness, Meaning, and Lasting Fulfillment in Your Life and Work, authors Timothy Keiningham and Lerzan Aksoy note that the shift away from long-term personal, familial, and work loyalty is "a natural by-product of the increasingly dynamic economic environment in which we live. We have become more flexible and more mobile workers, which has made businesses more efficient" (p. 5).[6]

While there are positive aspects to flexibility and mobility, Keiningham and Aksoy observe that these qualities also seem to contribute to the loss of loyalty because an employee (or employer) can easily move from position to position or even leave the company to go to a competitor in the same field or a different field altogether. One has only to look at NetJets, headquartered in Columbus, Ohio. In April and May 2015, the three top executives, including the CEO, resigned. The company was in disarray for a short time, but it quickly regrouped and offered the CEO and president positions to two of the top executives who had resigned if they returned to the company. Both of these executives had already accepted positions with other corporations, but they both returned to NetJets. (Gearino, 2015, pp.

Today, people can work almost anywhere.

CI-C-5).[7] As you consider this situation, think of the concept of loyalty not only to NetJets but also to the two other companies that had hired these executives from NetJets (although neither had yet started working for their new companies).

Until recently in human history, people needed to demonstrate a high degree of loyalty simply to survive; there was safety in numbers. Trying to live in isolation from others was extremely dangerous, and not having others around to take care of you in times of illness or crisis was tantamount to a death sentence. Keiningham and Aksoy observe that, in contrast, today individuals risk very little if they decide to leave a group with which they are affiliated (p. 6), as evidenced in the NetJets situation. The prosperity of our society provides most of us with a variety of employment opportunities and a social safety net of educational, healthcare, and support services that protect us from the worst of life's potential disasters. This, in turn, lessens the sense that we need to remain loyal to our friends, families, and organizations.

Columbia University law professor George Fletcher agrees, stating, "Today, we think about relatives, employers, religious groups, and nations the way we think about companies that supply us with other products and services. If we don't like what we are getting, we consider the competition."[8] In essence, we "vote with our feet." If you don't like the way your spouse squeezes the toothpaste tube, you can just get a divorce. If you don't like the way your boss treated you today, you can start looking for another job (or simply quit).

This freedom of mobility and choice is great for us in terms of the many paths and options it offers. We have opportunities today that people of 100, 50, or even 10 years ago never imagined. But what gets left behind with all this freedom is the sense of belonging and community that is the foundation of loyalty. The more "me"-focused we become, the less "we"-focused we are. No wonder loyalty is one of the things we admire most in our furry friends.

LOYALTY IN ACTION

Stories like that of Sallie and the soldiers of the 11th Pennsylvania, which illustrate the loyalty of dogs to their human counterparts, are more numerous than we can count. But one of the more famous (and poignant) is a wonderful tale about an Akita in Japan named Hachiko. Hidesaburo Ueno brought Hachiko to Tokyo in

---

7   Gearino, D. (2015, June 2). CEO takes flight. Columbus, OH: *The Columbus Dispatch*, pp. C-1-C-5.

8   Cited in Keiningham, T. & Aksoy, L. (2010). *Why Loyalty Matters: The Groundbreaking Approach to Rediscovering Happiness, Meaning and Lasting Fulfillment in Your Life and Work*. BenBella Books, Dallas, TX, p. 6.

1924. Every day, when Ueno left for his teaching job, Hachiko would stand by the door and watch him go—and each day, at 4:00 p.m., the Akita would go to Shibuya Station to meet his owner as he got off the train so they could walk home together.

A year after they arrived in Tokyo, Ueno died of a stroke while at work. He was not there when Hachiko went to meet him at the train station. Hachiko returned to the train station day after day at 4:00 p.m., searching for his owner's face amid the passengers getting off the train. Eventually, the stationmaster made the dog a bed at the station and began leaving him bowls of food and water. Hachiko returned to that train station every day for ten years until he died in 1935—but, in a way, the devoted dog remains at the station to this day. A year before his death, Shibuya Station installed a bronze statue of Hachiko, and although the original statue was melted down during World War II, a new version was created in 1948 by the original artist's son. In 2009, this touching story was even made into a movie, *Hachi: A Dog's Tale*, starring Richard Gere and Joan Allen.[9]

The famed Hachiko statue at Shibuya Station.

There is also the story of Miguel Guzmán of Argentina, who bought a dog, Capitán, for his son Damián in 2005. Capitán and the elder Guzmán became inseparable. When Guzmán died in 2006, Capitán suddenly vanished. No one knew where he had gone until a week after the funeral, when the family returned to the cemetery and found Capitán there, howling. The heartbroken dog had found

9   *Hachi: A Dog's Tale.* (2010, March 10). Los Angeles, CA: Stage 6 Studios.

A statue of Hachiko and Ueno stands at the University of Tokyo's agriculture department, where Ueno taught.

the cemetery on his own and stayed there, sleeping each night on his owner's grave. When Damián was interviewed by La Voz del Interior newspaper in 2012, when he was thirteen years old, he told reporters that he'd tried to bring Capitán home several times, but the dog always returned to the cemetery. Damian doesn't mind, though. "If he wants to stay there, it's fine ... he's taking care of my dad."[10]

Those of us who have dogs are gratefully aware of the years of unwavering loyalty they share with us. When we interviewed veterinarian Erin Newport, we learned that she has many wonderful stories about pets and their people, but one that is particularly moving is about her own dog, Bonnie, a Boxer that Newport chose from a litter when the pup was just three days old.

Newport said, "I was able to take her from her mom at eight weeks of age, and our journey began. To put it mildly, she was a handful, but with patience and training, she became a wonderful family dog. Bonnie assigned herself as the nanny for my first son, sleeping under his bassinet and constantly watching over him as he grew. She did the same with my second son. Many times, we had to protect her from the rambunctious boys!"

Through the years, Bonnie calmed down and was a constant companion to Erin and the boys. "When my husband and I divorced," Newport said, "Bonnie seemed

10   Argentinian Dog Stays by His Master's Grave for Six Years. (2013, September 13). Retrieved from www.nydailynews.com/news/world/argentinian-dog-stays-master-grave-years-article-1.1159250

to know when her affection was needed and supported me through many sad and lonely times with her sweet nature and nurturing disposition."

Unfortunately, Bonnie developed Addison's disease, which Newport diagnosed after the dog went into acute renal failure and her kidneys shut down for three days. Newport had to decide on a set time when they would have to let Bonnie go if she didn't show signs of improvement. Within just thirty minutes of the designated time, Bonnie urinated. She would be OK. "She never gave up," Newport said.

With medication and care, Bonnie lived with Addison's disease for four years until she stopped responding to her medication. Newport had to pause before continuing with the next part of her story: "Bonnie had been declining, and one Friday night in May, I could tell she was going downhill quickly but trying to hide it from me. I knew I would probably have a difficult decision to make the next morning. I awoke the next day to find her lying in the yard, very weak. I got her back into the house and started making calls to cancel my day of appointments at my veterinary hospital. Bonnie seemed comfortable, so I did not feel the need to hurry the process—and, as a veterinarian, I also knew that no heroics were going to make a difference this time."

Newport sat with Bonnie and cried for her, for herself, and for her boys. Bonnie was another important piece of the life that she and her boys had known. "At around 2:00 in the afternoon," Newport said, "I felt that I needed to get outside and away from the situation for a bit. I puttered around in the yard for about thirty minutes. When I returned to Bonnie's side, she raised her head and gave me the most endearing look, as if to say, 'You will be fine, Mom.' She then laid her head in my lap and took her last breath. She had waited to say goodbye to me!"

Newport continued, "Bonnie taught me a lesson in the type of loyalty that I have rarely seen from other humans: always try to give more in life than you take. As I [tell this story], I am smiling through my tears remembering Bonnie the Boxer— one of the best dogs ever!!"[11]

There is no doubt that dogs demonstrate loyalty of the purest kind—the type of loyalty we could use more of in our families, friendships, and business associations. So, how can we take the lessons in loyalty we learn from our furry friends and apply them to our own lives?

---

11   Interview with Dr. Erin Newport, May 22, 2013.

Personal Activity 2:

LOYALTY

Take a few minutes to think about what you have learned about loyalty from your dog (or other pet). In the space below, write a few of your thoughts to help you apply these lessons to your daily personal life and your business life.

Notes:

LOYALTY WITH FAMILY AND FRIENDS

What does it mean to say that we're loyal to our friends and family? In addition to being there for them when they need it, it means that we stick up for them even when they're not around. We've all been guilty of gossiping about someone who is not present. In his book, The Seven Habits of Highly Effective People, Dr. Stephen Covey says, "One of the most important ways to manifest integrity is to be loyal to those who are not present. In doing so, we build trust with those who are present."[12] Dr. Covey observes that when you are appropriately loyal to someone who is not present, other people observe your behavior, thus letting them know that you likewise will be loyal to them when they are not present. If, on the other hand, you quickly join in to gossip about someone else, those present know that you will also talk about them behind their backs.

Loyal friends and family are also genuinely happy—not resentful—about the good things that occur in your life. They listen when you talk and try to understand what you're saying rather than interpreting and judging. Loyal friends

---

12   Covey, S. (1989). *The Seven Habits of Highly Effective People.* New York: Simon and Schuster, p. 196.

and family will tell you (tactfully and diplomatically) what you need to hear instead of the things they think you want to hear.

Furthermore, true friends and family accept you for who you are, flaws and all, just like your dog does. When we come home tired and grumpy from a long day of work, our dogs are just as elated to see us as they would be if we'd arrived bearing a bag of treats. Can you say that you show the same appreciation for your loved ones day in and day out?

LOYALTY AT WORK AND IN BUSINESS

Loyalty, as we have seen, means the willingness to put someone else before you without conditions or requirements. Just as dogs display their loyalty to their human families, so should business owners and employees strive to be more loyal to each other. It's not just a matter of human decency; it also makes good business sense. The benefits of loyalty in the workplace are many, for both business leaders and employees. Loyal employees who strive to do their best at all times, get work accomplished, and look out for the company's interests are essential to the success of a business. When employees feel little to no loyalty to each other or the business, it's an "every person for him- or herself" atmosphere, which is detrimental to employees, the workplace environment, and the bottom line.

But, loyalty goes both ways. It is hard to feel loyalty toward a company or manager who is not loyal to you. So while employees should strive to be more loyal to those who provide them with a paycheck, companies also need to learn to treat their employees with the respect and empathy they deserve. One excellent example of a business owner who went above and beyond the call of duty to demonstrate loyalty to his employees was Aaron Feuerstein. Feuerstein was the owner of Malden Mills, a textile company that was known for going out of its way for its employees. In the winter of 1995, a fire broke out at Malden Mills, and the entire factory burned to the ground. While no one was injured, the town was distraught at the loss of one of its largest employers. "Experts" recommended that Feuerstein collect the $300 million in insurance and retire. Aaron recognized the impact that the loss of the factory would have on employees and the community, and he decided to rebuild the factory and continue to pay employees for the sixty days following the fire.

Eight years after the fire, Feuerstein was asked if he would reconsider his decision. "I think it was a wise business decision, but that isn't why I did it," Feuerstein replied. "I did it because it was the right thing to do."[13]

Most CEOs would agree that the long-term success of a company depends on the quality and loyalty of its workforce. Yet while few corporate executives would disagree with this idea conceptually, many treat the economic value of employees in enhancing customer relationships and company profits as "soft" numbers (numbers that don't make as much of an impact), unlike the "hard" numbers they use to manage their operations, such as sales and the cost of labor.

The problem with this type of short-term thinking is that when the going gets tough—and in the nature of business cycles, it most certainly will—managers focus on the hard numbers. The result is that in today's organizational climate, employees are besieged with a constant stream of downsizings and reorganizations. The layoff of hundreds (or thousands) of loyal employees make the front pages of our newspapers on a regular basis. And while Wall Street appears to view the layoff of employees as a sign that companies are getting their financial houses in order, the reality is quite different. Research shows that most

13   The Mensch of Malden Mills: CEO Aaron Feuerstein puts employees first. (2003, July 3). Retrieved from www.cbsnews. com/news/the-mensch-of-malden-mills/

organizations that undergo downsizing actually fail to realize any long-term cost savings or efficiencies, which, unfortunately, often suggests to senior management that even more restructurings and layoffs are needed.[14]

With layoffs occurring across numerous industries, it's no surprise that employees are asking, "Is there any loyalty left in the workplace?" It is a fair question. For employees, feeling valued and secure in one's job is often a thing of the past. Fortunately, there is evidence that loyalty is still alive in the workplace and that there are clear benefits for those organizations that display greater loyalty to their employees.

The Loyalty Research Center, an Indianapolis-based firm focusing on customer and employee loyalty, defines loyalty in part as "employees being committed to the success of the organization and believing that working for this organization is their best option." Simply put, loyal employees are often those who are most engaged. An engaged employee is one who is enthusiastic about his or her work and strives to further the organization's interests. Gallup, Inc. has conducted extensive research into employee engagement since 2000 and learned that loyalty is a key component. The results of this research indicate that employees fall into three groups:

---

14   Declining Employee Loyalty: A Casualty of The New Workplace. (2015, March 15). Retrieved from http://knowledge. wharton.upenn.edu/article/declining-employee-loyalty-a-casualty-of-the-new-workplace/

1. "Engaged" employees who are "emotionally attached to their workplaces and motivated to be productive";
2. "Not engaged" employees who are "emotionally detached and unlikely to be self-motivated"; and
3. "Actively disengaged" employees who "view their workplaces negatively and are liable to spread that negativity to others."[15]

The Gallup research results clearly indicate that organizations with a high percentage of engaged employees reap substantial benefits. For instance, organizations with high levels of engagement report 22 percent greater productivity, lower turnover among employees, fewer safety incidents, and fewer quality issues.[16] So, if loyalty in the workplace has advantages to both an organization and its employees, the obvious question is: What can be done to enhance loyalty? Let's start with what the organization can do, because, as Wharton management Professor Adam Cobb explains, "When you are talking about loyalty in the workplace, you have to think about it as a reciprocal exchange. My loyalty to the firm is contingent on my firm's loyalty to me. But there is one party in that exchange [that] has tremendously more power, and that is the firm."[17]

15   The State of The American Workplace: Employee Engagement Insights for U.S. Business Leaders. (2013). Retrieved from www.gallup.com/services/178514/state-american-workplace.aspx

16   Retrieved from https://hbr.org/2013/07/employee-engagement-does-more/

17   Declining Employee Loyalty: A Casualty of The New Workplace. (2015, March 15). Retrieved from http://knowledge.wharton.upenn.edu/article/declining-employee-loyalty-a-casualty-of-the-new-workplace/

ORGANIZATIONAL LOYALTY

The foundation of true loyalty lies in knowing that you can count on the other party in a relationship. Thus, trust is crucial. Research into organizational leadership and performance suggests that there are six essential steps an organization can take to demonstrate its loyalty and build trust with employees.[18]

The first step in building employee loyalty is to demonstrate employer loyalty by creating and sustaining meaningful channels of communication with employees. This step falls completely in line with one of the key tenets of good leadership; namely, that great leaders communicate, communicate, communicate.

Second, in today's dynamic business environment, change is both necessary and inevitable. Leaders in any organization need to continually seek ways to improve their work processes, products, and procedures if they are to be more efficient, cost effective, and competitive. Achieving efficient change means having employees who are always on the lookout for ways to improve their work in a manner that supports organizational growth. After all, employees are on the front line, whether they work in manufacturing or serve as the organization's face to its customer. It stands to reason that they will be in the best position to identify and report opportunities to enhance efficiency and productivity.[19]

To ensure that employees understand where the company is going and how to help it improve, it is important that employees understand the organization's mission and strategy. This is more than just having the CEO send out an e-mail or make a speech. It means making sure that employees understand how they fit into the big picture and how what they do every day contributes to organizational success.

Third, the organization needs to make sure that it is doing all it can to ensure that employees have the knowledge, skills, and resources they need to do their jobs well.[20] Employees want to be competent in their jobs. In order to empower them to do this, companies must invest time, money, and attention into providing the education and training employees need to excel. This may mean providing and encouraging employees to pursue further education or advanced degrees in subjects that would benefit the company. It may mean providing employees with on-site training, coaching, or mentoring on key job skills.

We know how important basic training is with our dogs; a well-trained dog

---

18   Durkin, D. M. (2004). *Loyalty in the Workplace*. Advance for Medical Laboratory Professionals, pp. 1-3.
19   *Ibid.*
20   *Ibid.*

understands our expectations and is able to work with us much more effectively than one who has to guess what we want from him. For example, when we get a new puppy or dog, we begin his life with us by giving him a tour of his new surroundings and often some guidelines about where he can (and can't) sit, jump up, etc.

Communicating clear expectations not only guarantees greater success; it makes both parties much happier. Just as we should communicate what we expect from our dogs or other pets, it only stands to reason that managers should do the same for their employees. This should also apply to upper management when someone is promoted to a position of more authority and has had very little training or mentoring for what the new position requires of him or her. This is further explained in the next paragraph.

Fourth, organizations must ensure that their supervisors and managers are trained and coached in basic supervisory and advanced management skills.[21] James Harter, chief scientist for workplace management and well-being at the Gallup organization, states quite clearly how important it is to develop employee loyalty: "If you're looking for a silver bullet, it is the quality of the relationship between an employee and his or her manager that determines the overall level of employee engagement."[22] Wharton management professor Matthew Bidwell agrees: "Employees are often more loyal

Whether training or playing, it's all about communication.

---

21   Ibid.

22   Retrieved from http://knowledge.wharton.upenn.edu/article/declining-employee-loyalty-a-casualty-of-the-new-workplace/

to those around them—their manager, their colleagues, maybe their clients. These employees have a sense of professionalism—and loyalty—that relates to the work they do more than to the company."[23]

The fifth step that organizations must take to build employee loyalty is to actively recognize and reward good performance.[24] This is a principle that we all know but often do not put in place within organizational settings. Parents know that they need to provide positive reinforcement to their children for demonstrating the right behaviors. Dog owners know the importance of giving their dogs a treat or a scratch behind the ears and making a positive fuss over them when they display desired behaviors. Giving frequent pats on the back to employees for consistent good work and effort is no different and can go a long way.

Garry recently led a group of executives from a multinational company in a strategic team-building retreat. One of the key insights they realized on this retreat was that most of their projects took twelve to eighteen months to complete and were very intensive in scope and development. Both employees and managers experienced a great deal of stress over these months due to shifting customer priorities, the need to keep pace with technology, and the personal challenges of working with team members based throughout the world. At one point during the retreat, one of the executives said, "While we do celebrate the success of a project, by the end, everyone is so beaten down and tired, they don't care anymore. Plus,

23   *Ibid.*.
24   Durkin, D.M. (2004). *Loyalty in the Workplace.*

they are already gearing up for a brand-new project."[25] As a result of the retreat, the executives resolved to identify key milestones at three- to six-month intervals for each project and to celebrate those as well—not just the end of the project.

In Garry's job as a university administrator, he tries to keep this same principle in mind and demonstrates his appreciation for the work of other individuals or departments with thoughtful gestures, such as a hand-delivered giant chocolate-chip cookie with "Thanks!" written on it in icing. It's a simple way of showing gratitude that also serves as public recognition of the effort that others have put forth.

Likewise, when Sharon's publishing team has completed a textbook project, she takes the entire team out for a lunch at a local restaurant of the team's choice. She caps off lunch with a treat from a local bakery: a cake baked to look like the book itself, frosted in a color that matches the textbook's cover and with the book's cover image on top (and the "icing on the cake" is that it is all edible!). Sharon also invites the author(s) to come and share in the celebration.

The sixth and final step that organizations can take to demonstrate and build loyalty is to provide continuous (and genuine) feedback on performance and professional development.[26] The best athletes are those who are open to constant feedback on what they're doing well, how they're doing in comparison to the competition, and what they need to do to improve. Employees need the same sort of clear, actionable feedback. (Not surprisingly, this ties closely with the previously mentioned step 4.) Taking the time to show an employee how he or she can be better demonstrates a genuine interest in the employee's progress and a desire to see him or her achieve.

Supervisors and managers need to understand how to conduct positive, constructive conversations with employees in order to help them understand what they're doing well, how their work contributes to (or detracts

25   Strategic Planning Retreat, Camp Mary Orton, Columbus, Ohio, July 22, 2011.

26   Durkin, D.M. (2004) *Loyalty in the Workplace*.

Personal Activity 3:

LOYALTY

Think of some situations you have witnessed in which loyalty to the organization was exemplified in a positive way by you and/or others in the organization. What do you think motivated the individuals to act with loyalty in these situations? What impact did this loyalty have on employees, the organization, and customers?

Notes:

from) the success of the work unit, and what they need to do to improve. A key element of this step is development. Good managers and supervisors recognize that their best employees will often "outgrow" their current positions. This means keeping an eye open for ways to help that individual move into more responsible and challenging positions within the company, even if it means losing the person from your team. Remember—part of loyalty is about doing what's best for others, not necessarily what is best for you.

EMPLOYEE LOYALTY

The other side of developing loyalty at work is what you as an employee can do to enhance relationships and trust with others within your work group and other units. However, before we go any further, let's understand that we are not talking about blind loyalty to one's organization or the people in it. Blind loyalty can lead to going along with something even if it goes against the law, organizational policies and procedures, or your own personal morals or integrity. That said,

some of the most honorable and admirable characteristics appreciated by coworkers are seen in the employee who is competent at his or her job and loyal to those with whom he or she works. What can you do to enhance and sustain your own loyalty at work?

First, you should be willing to sacrifice and make time for others who need help. In today's "do more with less" work culture, it is not uncommon for a supervisor or a coworker to need a little extra help. Yet, too often, employees who have some free time do not make the effort to help their colleagues. Don't wait to be asked; instead, volunteer. "Hey, you seem to have a lot going on right now. Is there anything I can do to help?" This may entail staying late, completing a task you don't particularly care for, or offering up resources to someone who needs them more than you do. The upside of these actions is that they're likely to result in reciprocal behavior, creating a mutual sense of loyalty between the two of you.

Second, make an effort to understand the challenges and opportunities that your coworkers, work unit, and organization face. The Gallup poll referenced earlier showed that, on average, 71 percent of employees are "not engaged" or are "actively disengaged."[27] By definition, this means that almost three-quarters of your colleagues are showing up for work, doing their jobs (maybe), and going home. You should want to be among the top 30 percent of employees who stand out by being more engaged.

27   The State of The American Workplace: Employee Engagement Insights for U.S. Business Leaders. (2013). Retrieved from (http://www.gallup.com/services/178514/state-american-workplace.aspx

In one of the classes that Sharon teaches, she has an ingenious way of recognizing the student who has stood out from the rest, has contributed regularly to class discussions, and has made a special effort to help his or her classmates. During the board presentations on the last night of class, she talks about the rockhopper penguin and how this species stands out from the rest in the penguin world. Rockhopper penguins are very distinctive, sporting beautiful crests of feathers over their eyes.

Sharon then calls the exemplary student up to the front of the class and presents him or her with a small rockhopper penguin figurine and explains why he or she is getting this award. It is amazing how much these students cherish their penguins; I often see the small rockhopper penguins sitting on the dashboards of students' cars.

As an employee, if you want your organization to be loyal to you, make an extra effort to ask questions, listen to discussions in meetings, and understand the concerns of your supervisor and coworkers. When you do not understand something, tactfully and diplomatically ask questions. Make a point of looking at issues from others' points of view. Remember that just because you can't see a budding problem or opportunity at work does not mean that someone else may not have a better perspective. Offer suggestions for solving problems when appropriate.

Third, be sure to make a concerted effort to extend your appreciation and thanks to your colleagues and supervisors when they've done an excellent job or helped you out with something. Some employees forget that supervisors need to be recognized

for their efforts, too. We are not talking about "kissing up"; we are suggesting that there's nothing wrong with honestly telling another person—at any level—how much you appreciate something they've done.

With your colleagues, demonstrate that you do not need to compete, but that you can instead find pleasure in celebrating their accomplishments as well as yours. It only takes a few minutes to reach out to your coworkers and show them that you care. Our dogs are never "too busy" to offer you comfort or to recognize how great you are. In fact, our pets can sometimes even be a little "clingy" in showing us affection and how happy they are just to be with us each day. (We are not suggesting that you follow your coworkers around adoringly like your well-meaning pet does. Try to strike a healthy balance between too much attention and not enough.)

Finally, follow through on what you say you will do. Show others that you are the type of person they can count on and will be there for them when needed. Be someone others can confide in—and, if they do, keep their comments confidential.

ONE FINAL TALE OF LOYALTY

Loyalty is a lot like love; it's not something you get, but something you give. And the great thing about loyalty is that, over time, it develops and leads to relationships that are profoundly satisfying—and, sometimes, even lifesaving.

One of the most moving stories of loyalty we've encountered is that of Omar Rivera, a computer technician who was employed on the seventy-first floor of the

World Trade Center's north tower on September 11, 2001. On that fateful day, Rivera, who is blind, was at his computer technician job with his guide dog, Salty, under his desk. When the two hijacked airplanes hit the Twin Towers, Rivera knew it would take a long time to get out of the building.

"I thought I was lost forever," he says. "The noise and the heat were terrifying. But I had to give Salty the chance of escape. So I unclipped his lead, ruffled his head, gave him a nudge, and ordered Salty to go."

Salty was swept downstairs by the vast crowd of people rushing to escape. Yet, a few minutes later, Rivera felt the dog nuzzling his legs—he had pushed his way back up the crowded staircase to his owner! Salty and a coworker helped Rivera climb down seventy flights of stairs, a trip that took more than an hour. Shortly after they finally emerged at ground level, the building collapsed. Rivera declares that he owes his life to his companion and loyal friend, Salty.[28]

Loyalty is a choice, just like any other noble habit, and if we truly believe it is worthwhile and valuable, we can choose to demonstrate it every day—by building stronger, more devoted relationships with our family, friends, coworkers, and employees that lead to a greater sense of safety, security, and closeness.

In your own words, define what loyalty means to you.

What actions do you need to take to be a more loyal friend and/or to choose friends who are more loyal to you? What benefit(s) will that bring to you and others?

What actions do you need to take to be a more loyal family member and/or for a family member to be more loyal to you? How will you all benefit?

Describe what you believe it means to be loyal as an employee where you work. Describe an employee who exhibits the traits we have discussed about loyalty. Describe another employee who fails to exhibit the majority of these traits, in your opinion. On what is your opinion based?

What actions do you need to take to be a more loyal employee, and how will you benefit?

If you are a manager or business owner, what does it mean for an organization to be loyal to employees, and how will you/the business benefit?

What actions do you and/or your business need to take to demonstrate greater loyalty to employees?

CHAPTER 2
COMMUNICATION

*You can say
any foolish thing to a dog,
and the dog
will give you a look
that says,
"Wow, you're right!
I never would've
thought of that!"*

—DAVE BARRY

One day, Garry was in his front yard playing with Panda when his neighbors, Liza and Paul, walked by with their two dogs: Shimano, a thirteen-year-old Husky mix, and Isi, their newest addition, a four-month-old yellow female Labrador Retriever puppy. With all the enthusiasm that only a puppy can bring, Isi immediately bounded down the sidewalk to meet her new friend, Panda, with Shimano slowly bringing up the rear as fast as his arthritic hips would allow. What occurred next was an example in effective communication. As Isi and Shimano approached, Panda halted in the yard, head and ears up, staring intently at the two dogs. His tiny stub of a tail was also as erect as it could go and wagging rapidly from side to side.

As Isi approached within the final few feet, she lowered her head and, with her tail wagging furiously, slunk toward Panda. Panda stood absolutely still as Isi dropped in front of him, rolled onto her back, and started pawing the air with her feet. When Panda did not growl or attack, Isi rolled back onto her feet and began to lick his face while dancing about in delight with her tail going full blast.

By this time, Shimano had arrived. Because he was an older dog, Shimano simply stood a couple of feet away, erect and looking at Panda and Isi with only a sideways glance every now and then and with his tail wagging slowly from side to side. With the puppy jumping, rolling, and leaping around him, Panda slowly approached Shimano, and the two tentatively

smelled each other's rears. With all of these "pleasantries" out of the way, Panda finally turned back to Isi and dropped his front paws to the ground in the classic "let's play" position. This was all Isi needed—a new "big dog" wanted to play with her! And they were off. Given his stiff hips, Shimano spent his time with a big doggy smile on his face, turning in circles as he watched the two younger dogs racing by, first in one direction and then in another.

We are sure you have also observed similar encounters between dogs. Dogs, like human beings, are highly social animals. During this chance meeting among Panda, Isi, and Shimano, the dogs exhibited a complex set of behaviors to ensure that their intentions and feelings were clearly understood. It is also why we suggest that being excellent communicators is another quality we admire in dogs.

Rather than simply accepting these authors' opinions, you might ask what other evidence suggests that human beings appreciate a dog's ability to communicate. Well, consider this: In 2004, the American Animal Hospital Association (AAHA) conducted an opinion survey of 1,238 pet owners in the United States and Canada.[1] While the surveyor's questions were posed with regard to all pets, 74 percent of respondents chose dogs as the pet for which they provided answers. When asked, "Who listens to you best?" It was: 45 percent responded that their pet is a better listener than their significant other. Think of it: more people

1   American Animal Hospital Association. (2004). Pet Owner Survey. Retrieved March 19, 2015, from https://www.aahanet. org/PublicDocuments/petownersurvey2004.pdf

responded that they believe their dog listens to them better than their best human companion! And if you think that is revealing, 40 percent of respondents said that if they were stranded on a deserted island with only one companion, they would pick their dog over a human being.

These results speak to a deep need that we all share. Human beings want and need to communicate effectively with others. The ability to communicate effectively is consistently cited as a key element that contributes to success in marriages, in relationships with children, and in the workplace. In their book, *Business Communication Today*, authors Bovée and Thill state, "Improving your communication skills may be the single most important step you can take in your career. You can have the greatest ideas in the world, but they're no good to your company or your career if you can't express them clearly and persuasively."[2]

In an article in *Forbes Magazine*, Mike Myatt supports this statement, noting that the ability to communicate is one of the greatest skills any leader can possess, that most organizational problems occur as a result of poor communication, and that effective communication is an essential component of professional success whether it is at the interpersonal, intergroup, intragroup, organizational, or external level.[3]

2   Bovée, C.L., & Thill, J. V. (2016). *Business Communication Today*. Pearson Education, NJ: Upper Saddle River, p. 4.
3   Myatt, M. (2012). 10 communication secrets of great leaders. *Forbes*, April 4, 2012. Retrieved March 19, 2015, from *www.forbes.com/sites/mikemyatt/2012/04/04/10-communication-secrets-of-great-leaders/*.

Not surprisingly, Inc. magazine, in an article published online in May 2010, notes that at the most basic level, employees who don't know what's expected of them seldom perform to their potential. "You can tie back almost every employee issue—attendance, morale, performance, and productivity—to communication," says Fred Holloway, a human-resources adviser in Medford, Oregon.[4] And good communication is vital for families as well. According to Sandra J. Bailey, PhD, CFLE, family and human development specialist with Montana State University, "Good family relations are built on strong communication. It creates and keeps strong family ties."[5]

WHAT IS GOOD COMMUNICATION?

Communication is "good" when you and I not only trade ideas, feelings, and information but also create and share meaning. Like dogs, we are social creatures interacting with others on a daily basis at work, school, on the phone, or at home with our families. Unfortunately, as you have no doubt experienced, sometimes our listening and speaking skills do not have the effect we hoped for. And in a world where there are more and more personal electronic devices clamoring for our attention every minute of the day and night, effective communication is becoming an even greater challenge. Fortunately, with a little knowledge, we can improve our communication skills and, in turn, improve how well we are understood by others both at work and at home.

As Panda, Isi, and Shimano demonstrated, dogs are masters of the habit of good communication. And as with the other secrets to happiness, we believe we can learn a great deal by examining what dogs do well and reflecting on how we can emulate their success. There are many books, audio programs, and speakers who describe the qualities of effective communication. However, if you want to get to the heart of the matter, there are three key factors that differentiate good communication from poor communication: the ability to pay attention, the ability to listen, and the ability to respond.

Consider a typical interaction between two dogs. When two dogs meet, they begin by paying attention to each other. Next, the dogs "listen" by observing each other's posture, size, gender, behavior, and vocalizations to understand the

4   Retrieved March 19, 2015, from www.inc.com/magazine/20100501/guidebook-how-to-communicate-with-employees.html/

5   Bailey, S. J. (2009, September). Positive family communication. Montana State University Extension MontGuide.

other's intentions. Finally, each dog responds in a manner that ensures the other dog understands his or her message through body and ear position, tail wagging, behavior, and vocalizations.

By paying attention to the other dog, listening to understand intent, and then responding with appropriate behavior, both dogs achieve a very precise level of mutual understanding, which we can observe based on whether they decide to play, ignore each other, or fight. Let me stress that unlike humans, dogs consistently and clearly communicate what they mean and act accordingly. As Garry confided, some years ago he had the opportunity to conduct a workshop in Moscow on the topic of high-performance leadership. One day, he and his wife were having lunch with their friend, Andrei, and Andrei asked what personal writing projects Garry was involved in. Garry mentioned that he was doing research for this book on dogs, and Andrei exclaimed, "Oh, I love dogs! Dogs have crystal hearts!" Garry asked him what he meant by this statement, and Andrei said, "A dog's heart is crystal-clear; there is no guile or deception. Dogs don't pretend to want to play and then attack. What they communicate is exactly what they intend."

Andrei went on to note that this is not the case for human beings. People frequently say one thing when we believe or intend something else. Or, we pretend that we are paying attention when we are actually thinking about something else.

If dogs can be effective communicators with us, doesn't it seem reasonable that we could be better communicators with each other? Let's look at how we can enhance our skills of paying attention, listening to understand, and responding appropriately, all with the goal of helping enhance the quality of our relationships with others.

PAY ATTENTION

Garry mentioned that he has a colleague at work who will drop in to talk about something of importance and then spend the entire time checking email and responding to text messages on his mobile phone. Garry has become very accustomed to this individual, who will say, "Go ahead and keep talking; I'm listening," when at the same time he is busily scrolling around his screen and typing with both thumbs. You know as well as I do that he is not paying attention and consequently is not able to listen effectively to what Garry has to say. How do we know this for certain? Because we are often guilty of the same infraction, and we are no more effective at focusing on another person while multitasking than Garry's coworker is.

Consider the situation at the beginning of this chapter, when we described and discussed how Panda reacted when he was approached by the neighbor's two dogs. Even though he and Garry had been playing in the yard together, Panda stopped and gave the approaching dogs his undivided attention. Panda was focused, and he communicated his friendly intentions through his body posture and wagging tail, telling the other two dogs that it was safe for them to approach him. While Panda was "reading" Isi's and Shimano's intentions by observing their body language as they approached, both the young puppy and her older playmate were focused on Panda. Panda observed that the puppy, Isi, "knew her place" and was appropriately subservient to him as a dominant male. Panda had also learned from previous encounters with the older dog that each needed only to communicate their equal status and good intentions.

As the respondents in the AAHA survey indicated, human beings view dogs as great communicators. In his book, *The Dog Who Couldn't Stop Loving*, Jeffrey Moussaieff Masson stresses that dogs also make a concerted attempt to focus on our behavior. He explains, "Dogs want to read us. They are constantly attempting to understand what we feel from how we look and our body language. Miraculously, they can often read us better than we can read ourselves. Hardly any other animal seems to care how we feel, and certainly no other animal is as alert to our emotions as dogs."[6] Masson explains that a dog makes a point of "fixing" on his master's or mistress's face and pays close attention to body language and gestures.

The importance of paying attention to another person is illustrated in part by the basic communication process described in many textbooks. I teach a class in our university's MBA program on the topic of business communication. In the first class, the students and I discuss how a message or idea travels from one person to another and then back again. This process is shown in Figure 2.[7]

First, I have an idea or thought to share with you. Second, I encode the idea—meaning that I put the thought into a message through words, actions, or pictures. In step 3, I transmit the message, or share it with you. Ideally, you receive it (step 4), and then in step 5, you decode, or interpret, the message. (Decoding is an important part of listening, which we will talk about next). Finally, in step 6 you respond to the message, and the dialogue continues as feedback to the sender in step 7.

The students correctly observed that while each step is important, if you leave any step out, the whole communication process suffers. For example, when

---

6   Masson, J.M. (2011). *The Dog Who Couldn't Stop Loving: How Dogs Have Captured Our Hearts for Thousands of Years*, New York: Harper Paperbacks, p. 62.

7   Bovee, C.L., & Thill, J. V. (2012). *Business Communication Today*. Upper Saddle River, NJ: Pearson Education, p. 10.

Garry tries to communicate with his colleague at work, and the colleague is busy reading and responding to messages on his phone, he is not focused on Garry and the message that Garry is trying to communicate. No matter how clearly and articulately Garry conveys the message, there's less of a chance that it will be received correctly. In this situation, the communication process has just run into a brick wall.

As Garry states hesitantly, he is not perfect and is also very guilty of not paying attention. For example, he was embarrassed to admit that, on some days, after a long day at work, when he gets home and flops down on the couch to watch the news, one of his children or his wife, Lauren, will try to share something of importance to their day. Garry says, "While I like to think I am a consummate professional at looking like I am paying attention (smiling, nodding, and glancing

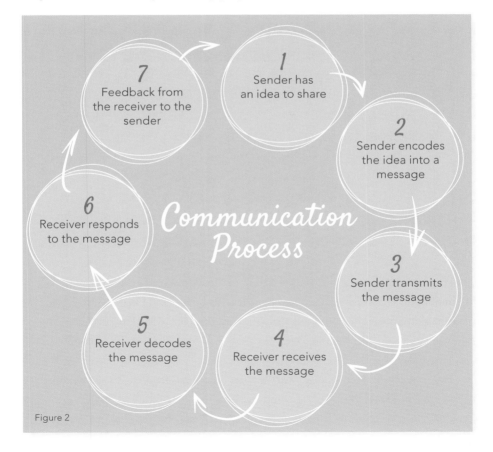

Figure 2

at them occasionally), I confess that I find it very easy to keep most of my attention on the television. I'll bet you are just as good at pretending to pay attention as I am. But you and I are not fooling anyone; others can see through our attempts to pretend to pay attention, and this damages the other person's trust in us and our relationship because that person feels minimized and ignored.

"It is important to recognize that paying attention is a choice. I have fallen into a bad habit of not paying attention when I honestly have the ability to do so. I haven't always failed to be highly focused and attentive when my wife communicated to me. When we were first married, my wife said that one of the qualities she most appreciated in me was that when she wanted to talk about something, I would stop what I was working on to focus on her. She knew from my behavior that I was paying attention. As you have no doubt noticed from the previous paragraph, my sense of focus has degraded a bit since then. Now, I can make excuses and blame my failure to communicate effectively with my wife and children on what I would like to believe is a much more demanding world. I can rationalize that there is always something else of legitimate importance that is vying for my attention. You know—kids needing help with homework, an exciting show on television, my wife wanting to tell me about her day, papers to grade, presentations to prepare, and, of course, Panda going out of his way to let me know he wants to play tug-of-war with his rope toy—all at the same time! I'm willing to bet that, like me, you could become an Olympic gold medal contender at being able to fake paying attention to another person while doing something else. The problem is that pretending to pay attention is not effective, and it is disrespectful. Frankly, I should be a better communicator—especially to those I love. So the foundation of the communication process for all of us is to stop what we are doing and pay attention to the other person."

Just as Garry shared his slip-up in paying attention at times, Sharon said the following: "I too have found myself losing out on important pieces of information being handed to me. Even my Miniature Schnauzer, Pup, had to find a way to bring me back to his reality when I drifted off into mine. He loved to spend time with me after dinner while I was grading papers; most of the time, he would be around somewhere, playing with a toy, glancing at me occasionally, nuzzling my leg, or even 'talking' to the TV.

"When he wanted my direct attention and I was lax in giving it, he made no mistake in letting me know his displeasure at my inattention. He had a habit that I had never seen so perfected in any dog as this one. He could spit a toy, a pill, or anything several feet with accuracy. So, my inattention would usually be halted by Pup's walking a few feet backward, holding a toy, a puppy chew bone, or something similar. He would then hold back his head and spit that object right into the middle of my lap! Pup would then stomp his right foot, turn his back in disgust, and storm off into another room, leaving me with a soggy object in my lap."

LISTEN

The second component to effective communication is to be a good listener. Listening is the process of both receiving a message and then accurately processing or "decoding" the message to make sense of it. If you are like most people, you go through your day doing some talking and some listening. However, are you really listening or just going through the motions as in Garry's example? Many of us are just going through the motions, and this may be for good reason: most of us have never been taught how to listen. For example, in working with organizations all over the world, it has been noted that people often have the opportunity to attend training or educational programs designed to teach them how to get their messages

across to others. These programs include professionally developed and often high-priced courses in sales, presentation, persuasion, and negotiation skills. But few people attend training to learn how to be more effective listeners.

Remember the results from the AAHA's survey? Close to half of the respondents noted that their dogs are better listeners than their significant others! Perhaps some of the reason why we do not listen more effectively is that we tend to leap to telling others what we think—and often before we understand what they are trying to say.

The importance people place on listening is illustrated in a compliment Garry received from one of his colleagues at the university. Garry relates that, one afternoon, he and his colleague were returning to campus after participating in a large community event when the colleague turned to Garry and said, "You know, I've noticed that people really like to talk to you. People come up to you, and, after a few minutes of conversation, they start sharing all kinds of information about the challenges and opportunities they are facing. You just look very interested and ask a question once in a while. Why don't you ever give them any advice?"

As you might guess from his last question, this faculty member is very action-oriented and is eager to tell others how to solve what he perceives as their problems.

As educators, we feel that it is more important to listen. We believe that most people can talk through their own issues and come to resolutions that work best for them. In other words, most people can solve their own problems and are just delighted when someone simply listens. When someone is assured that you are actually listening, he or she tends to open up and share even more.

If you are having a hard time accepting this point, consider that humans value dogs so much because they listen even though they don't understand what we are saying, and often because they don't provide advice or opinions. If you are having a bad day, you can count on your dog to sit with you and listen as you pour out your feelings. If you are having a great day and are excited about something, your dog is delighted to share in your joy.

Julianne Kaminski, a cognitive psychologist at the Max Planck Institute for Evolutionary Anthropology, states that the dog's ability to pay attention to what we have to say may be evolutionary. She explains, "We think that we are looking at a special adaptation in dogs to be sensitive to human forms of communication. There is … evidence suggesting that selection pressures during domestication have changed dogs such that they are perfectly adapted to their new niche, the human environment."[8]

To explore this phenomenon, Kaminski and her colleagues compared how well chimps and dogs understood human gestures and visual cues. In their experiment,

a person would point at an object that was out of his or her reach but within reach of the chimp or dog. If the animal retrieved the object, he was rewarded with a tasty food treat. Researchers were surprised to find that the chimps ignored the humans' gestures while the dogs aced the test, even when the human did not even look at the item to which he or she

8   Viegas, J. (2012, February 8.) Dogs really do understand us best. Retrieved March 19, 2015, from *http://news.discovery.com/animals/zoo-animals/dogs-humans-120208.html*

was pointing. Kaminski thinks that chimps simply have not evolved the ability to pay attention to humans in order to achieve a goal. Simply put, dogs pay attention to and comprehend what we are trying to communicate to them by watching our eyes and through our words and gestures.[9]

"Not listening" is one of the most common complaints we have about others, both at home and in our professional lives. People will tolerate a great deal of rude behavior, but when they feel that they are consistently not being listened to, they feel disrespected and insulted. The flip side of the coin is that when people feel that they are being listened to, they feel valued and appreciated.

Marshall Goldsmith, best-selling author and business consultant, suggests that one of the reasons we get so annoyed when others do not listen to us is that listening is something we know we should be able to do with ease.[10] He notes that the failure to listen sends out a host of negative messages, such as, "I don't care about you, what you have to say is not important to me, and you are wasting my time."[11]

Often, however, we are able to get away with not listening because it is easy to do so. You can look like you are listening even when you are bored, thinking about something else, or formulating your response while the other person is still talking.

9   Ibid.

10   Goldsmith, M. (2014, July 20). How to really listen. Retrieved March 20, 2015, from www.inc.com/marshall-goldsmith/how-to-really-listen.html (

11   Ibid.

BARRIERS TO LISTENING

Many years ago, Garry attended a lecture at the University of Texas at which nationally acclaimed correspondent Dan Rather spoke.[12] At the end of his lecture, Rather began to take questions from the audience. Among the attendees was a man who, when given the microphone, began a rambling statement interspersed with questions that were difficult to understand. People in the audience began to laugh, boo, and make loud comments to get the man to stop. Rather politely addressed the crowd, noting that the man had every right to ask his questions and state his opinions in the way that made sense to him. He went on to ask the audience to listen respectfully. After giving the man a chance to speak, Rather summed up the man's question and gave a thoughtful answer before moving on to take a question from another person.

Garry recalls, "Those of us in the audience that day had the opportunity to see a true listening professional in action. Dan Rather demonstrated why he is considered one of the best in his field by avoiding the barriers to listening to which most of us in the audience succumbed." What are the barriers that so often keep us from listening effectively?

12   Rather, D. (2009, October 22). Speaker at the Mary Alice Davis Distinguished Lectureship, University of Texas at Austin, School of Journalism

Personal Activity: Listening Barriers

Think about any barriers to listening that plague you and jot them down quickly here. Why do you think these particular barriers are difficult for you to overcome?

Notes:

First, it is easy for many of us to jump to conclusions and decide that we already know what the other person is going to say. Or, we might judge what the other person is saying as not important, boring, or difficult to understand. Therefore, it is easy to react as the crowd did in the aforementioned example and either harass the speaker or simply stop listening. As Mr. Rather showed, though, this is precisely where it is important to stay focused and listen for valuable ideas and information. Mr. Rather also made sure that he understood the man by summing up his question.

Second, in today's busy world, it is easy to fall victim to distractions. We are bombarded by personal communication devices and other interruptions that seem to vie for our attention. Effective listeners make a concerted effort to remain focused on the speaker by maintaining eye contact, ignoring their cell phones, or meeting to talk in a quiet place where there is less opportunity for disruption.

A third barrier to listening is our own emotions. When we feel strongly about a topic, it is easy for our emotional investment to distort what we hear or say. For example, if we are very excited about a topic, we may practice "selective listening," only hearing what fits with our expectations. In essence, we hear what we want to hear. On the other hand, because we are emotionally connected to our point of view, we can be overly defensive when others disagree or ask for clarity. To avoid overreacting, a good listener remembers that the goal of a conversation is to reach the best possible solution, not just his or her solution.

RESPOND

Two dogs meeting for the first time can size each other up in a very short period of time. Each first focuses his attention on the other and then "listens" to properly interpret the intentions of the other dog through the dog's posture, vocalizations, and behavior. The third step in the communication process is for each dog to respond appropriately.

The same is true for humans. By paying attention to another person and listening carefully, we can advance the conversation. To complete the effective communication cycle, we also need to respond in a way that demonstrates to the person that we did, in fact, hear and understand what he or she said.

Garry shared the following personal example about how a simple, well-intentioned conversation and what he thought was the correct response went off track. Early one morning, Garry's daughter called from school, saying that she had forgotten her backpack and asking if he could drop it off on his way to work. She also asked if Garry would bring the cookie sheet that she had left in the kitchen. Garry found her backpack in her room, where she said it would be, and, sure enough, there was a metal cookie sheet sitting on top of the stove. He took the cookie sheet and backpack to the school and met his daughter in the lobby. However, as Garry started to hand her the cookie sheet, she asked, "What's that for?" "What do you

mean?" he replied. "You told me to bring the cookie sheet; I assumed it was for a class project." Julie burst out laughing and said, "No! I meant my Girl Scout cookie sheet that lists all the people who have ordered cookies." Garry and his daughter had a laugh over this minor misunderstanding. (And, yes, he did have to run home, get the Girl Scout cookie sheet, and bring it back to school!)

Providing a correct response, as the example suggests, involves two important steps. The first step in responding is to ensure that you really understand the other person. The second step is to share your message. Let's look at these two steps one at a time.

The first step is to make sure that you have actually understood what the other person was trying to communicate. You can ensure understanding by paying attention to visual cues that indicate the other person's level of emotion, enthusiasm, or interest. You can also summarize or paraphrase what you believe you heard the other person say before you give your response. For example, when I was talking on the phone to my daughter, I could have checked my understanding by asking, "Do you want a round cookie sheet or a square one?" Had I done so, she could have immediately let me know that she did not mean a metal cookie sheet, but the list of people who had signed up to purchase Girl Scout cookies.

That would have saved me a second trip to the school and some degree of embarrassment.

The second step is to convey your message to the other person in a manner that enhances the probability that he or she will understand it as you intend. As we have seen, dogs know that how you communicate your message is as important as the message itself. It stands to reason that we should be developing these skills ourselves. Here are a couple of tips for ensuring that your message is received.

1. Once you have determined that you understood the other person, it is important to state your opinion or suggestions in a respectful manner. No one likes to feel that he or she is being disrespected, so avoid attacking the other person verbally or otherwise making the person feel as if you are putting him or her down.

2. Next, respond openly and honestly with an appropriate tone of voice. Share your thoughts, ideas, suggestions, or reactions with the other person in a way that is clear and easy to understand.

To bring this into current context, following is what one company is doing to be sure it understands the way its customers communicate:

Taco Bell executives are studying the language of their young customers in order to better understand its biggest fan base and how they communicate. Taco Bell conducts this research by featuring a "Millennial Word of the Week" at its headquarters. The CEO, Brian Niccol, said the words are "curated" by a group of employees in their twenties who send out an email every Tuesday or Wednesday. The words are also posted on screens and monitors around the office. For example, the word "lit," according to the definition given by Taco Bell, means that a "certain situation, person, place, or thing is awesome/crazy or just happening in general." To use it in a sentence: "The concert was so lit last night, I had to wait an hour to get in line." [13]

COMMUNICATING A POSITIVE MESSAGE

This all seems pretty simple, doesn't it? It would appear that all we have to do to become effective communicators is pay attention, listen, and respond effectively. However, there is one more aspect of communication, which we believe that dogs demonstrate, that is highly applicable to our lives as well: dogs are very careful

---

13   Retrieved from www.columbian.com/news/2015/jun/11/taco-bell-learning-lingo-of-its-millennial-custome/

about what they communicate. For the most part, unless a dog feels threatened, he communicates a very positive message.

How we communicate is important to us in both our professional and personal lives and can be understood by considering the work that psychologist and business consultant, Marcial Losada, conducted on the effect of positive to negative experiences in interpersonal interactions. Dr. Losada's research suggests that it takes about three meaningful positive comments or experiences to fend off the damaging effects of one negative comment or experience. If one dips below this tipping point (known as the "Losada Line"), the quality of interpersonal relationships and on-the-job performance declines quickly. He also suggests that if you rise above it (ideally at a ratio of six or more positive comments for each negative comment), relationships and performance are strengthened. This principle applies not only to what we say or do to others but also to how we talk to ourselves, which can have significant effects on one's level of happiness.

Thus, you might find it interesting to think about how you have talked to yourself and to others over the past week. If you can't recall, then you might find it well worth your time to observe this trend over the next week. What is the ratio of positive to negative comments you make about yourself? For example, do you give yourself positive messages about that which you are capable of doing, or do you give

yourself messages that doubt your abilities, appearance, and so on? You can expand this to consider how you communicate with others. To this end, what is your ratio of positive and supporting comments to friends, loved ones, and associates? What can you do to enhance the ratio of positive to negative comments? What impact do you think it will have if you share more frequent, real, positive comments to others for whom you care?

Let's look at an example of how the Losada Line might play out in the real world. When Garry was in college, he had to work twenty to thirty hours a week to pay for tuition and other living expenses. One semester, Garry took a position at a local pizza parlor. Each morning at 6 a.m., he and another student would fold pizza boxes and prepare balls of dough that could be quickly rolled out into pizzas for the coming day. Every morning, around 7:30, the owner of the pizzeria would arrive and begin a nonstop tirade about how badly the two boys made dough, how slow they were at folding boxes, and how much better every other worker he had ever hired had done their jobs. Because Garry and his coworker were making the desired number of boxes and the pizza dough balls using the recipe the owner had provided, they were puzzled at this consistent criticism.

Garry relates that he even asked on several occasions if the owner could show them what they were doing wrong or how to improve. In each case, the owner failed to provide any improvement suggestions but continued to complain that the two boys were not working as fast and hard as he thought they should. Garry also notes that at no time during his employment at the pizza parlor did he ever hear this gentleman give a positive compliment to any employee. Not even something as innocuous as, "You are still too slow, but you are a lot faster than you were last week. I can see the improvement." After enduring this haranguing for five mornings a week for two weeks, Garry made the profoundly wise decision to quit.

Our point in sharing this story is that great leaders are also great communicators. Great leaders know that what you say and how you say it are both important. This is true at both home and at work. If you talk to others in angry, negative tones, you handicap their willingness to listen. Dr. Losada has decades' worth of research suggesting that in work teams, a ratio of positive to negative interaction of 3:I is necessary to ensure the team's success.[14] This means that it takes it three positive comments, experiences, or expressions to counterbalance the effects of just one negative comment. Losada maintained that if the ratio dipped below 3:I, productivity, morale, and performance would drop. His research also shows that high-performing teams produce their best work when the ratio is 6:I.

14   Retrieved March 15, 2015, from http://positivepsychologynews.com/news/marcial-losada/200812091298.

Losada's research also suggested that organizations could improve in productivity, sales, and morale when leaders are trained and held responsible for providing more positive feedback to employees and work teams.[15] If true, this formula for the impact of communication on others would also be applicable to families. So, you might ask yourself: if your interactions at home with your spouse, significant other, and/or children were observed, what would be the ratio of positive to negative comments or interactions? What impact might it have on workplace performance and interpersonal relationships if you simply engaged in more frequent, genuine, and positive interactions?

Buddy, Isi, Shimano, Panda, and other dogs clearly demonstrate the three basic skills of effective communication: paying attention, listening, and responding— and they communicate a very consistent positive message. Whether it is through verbal or nonverbal communication, life is ultimately about relationships—that is, with your family, friends, coworkers, employees, clients, customers, and everyone else with whom you interact. All the talent in the world means very little if you are not able to communicate effectively with others. So take this habit to heart and learn to communicate as effectively with others as your dog does with you.

15   Ibid.

HOW GOOD ARE YOUR LISTENING SKILLS?

Answer each question below as honestly as you can, using the 5-point scale. Circle the number that corresponds most closely with how you would answer that question.

I frequently try to listen to several conversations at the same time.	1 2 3 4 5
I like people to give me only the facts and then let me figure out what they meant.	1 2 3 4 5
Sometimes I pretend to pay attention to others when they are talking.	1 2 3 4 5
I am very good at reading other people's non-verbal communications.	1 2 3 4 5
I can tell what another person is going to say before he or she says it.	1 2 3 4 5
If a conversation does not interest me, I find something else to think about.	1 2 3 4 5
I frequently nod my head, smile, or frown to show the other person I am paying attention.	1 2 3 4 5
I usually respond immediately when another person has finished talking.	1 2 3 4 5
I evaluate what is being said while the other person is still talking.	1 2 3 4 5
I usually formulate a response to what a person is saying while he or she is still talking.	1 2 3 4 5
I find that other people's style of communication makes it hard for me to pay attention.	1 2 3 4 5
I usually ask other people to clarify what they have said rather than taking a guess at what I think they meant.	1 2 3 4 5
I try very hard to ensure I am focusing on understanding other people's point of view.	1 2 3 4 5
I frequently hear what I expect to hear instead of what the other person really said.	1 2 3 4 5
Most people would say I understood their point of view even if we disagree.	1 2 3 4 5

1 = Strongly Agree 2 = Agree 3 = Neutral 4 = Disagree 5 = Strongly Disagree

Scoring: Sum up your responses for all questions; however, reverse your scores for questions 4, 12, 13, and 15 (5 = 1 point, 4 = 2 points, 3= 3 points, 2 = 4 points, 1 = 5 points)

Adapted from Glenn, E.C., & Pood, E.A. (1989, January) Listening Self-Inventory, *Supervisory Management*, pp. 12-15.

with a bunch of friends? Did you have a tree house to which you could escape and where playful mischief abounded? Maybe you loved to play cowboy and gallop around the yard on a pretend stallion, or you went to the swimming pool and played "Marco Polo" until you were exhausted.

Ah, those were the days, weren't they? The question you need to ask yourself is: What are you doing to reconnect with your inner puppy? In this chapter, we are going to explore what you can do to stay in touch with your inner sense of play and adventure.

Humans are born to play, and we often describe "playing" as times in our lives when we feel most alive, yet we often take the value of play for granted. Joe Robinson, author of *Don't Miss Your Life* (Wiley, 2010), stresses that playfulness is not a character defect; rather, it is how we build character and develop persistence, competence, and social skills that push us beyond our perceived limits.[1] From this point of view, play is not a luxury; it is an absolute necessity for enhancing our ongoing development from the time we are kids, through adulthood, and even into our elderly years. Playing is how we learn, how we expand our bodies and minds, and often how we express ourselves. Through play, we learn important lessons about life as well as how to free our energy, joyfulness, and imaginations.

1   Robinson, J. (2011, January 18). The Key to Happiness: A Taboo for Adults? *Huffington Post*. Retrieved from www.huffingtonpost.com/joe-robinson/why-is-the-key-source-of-_b_809719.html

Despite the amazing value and power of play, somewhere between childhood and adulthood, many of us stop playing. We exchange the joy of play we experienced as children for the world of work and responsibility. When we do have some leisure time, we are often inclined to simply become passive receptors of entertainment by watching television or a movie. During our travels, we often see people "on vacation" who simply can't tear themselves away from the office. You can go to the most wonderful tropical paradise, wander out to the cabana, and see a dozen people pounding away on their laptops, answering emails, and talking to the office on their cell phones while everyone else is having a great time in the pool or at the beach, only yards away. You have heard the excuses: "I don't have anyone back in the office I can count on," or "If I don't stay in touch, I will have a million emails and voicemails when I get back." Loehr and Schwartz, in their book, *The Power of Full Engagement* (Free Press, 2003), reflect on this paradox, stating, "We live in a world that celebrates work and activity, ignores renewal and recovery, and fails to recognize that both are necessary for sustained high performance."[2]

Having said this, it is perhaps important to note that there are some people who work on vacation or elsewhere when not at the office because they enjoy this quiet time for doing work. They feel happy at having accomplished a lot more at home or away than they may have at the office on a general day because, at the office, last-minute tasks and emergencies seem to crop up unannounced.

On the other hand, dogs appear to understand the value of a balanced life, which includes eating, sleeping, work, and play. Unfortunately, as we grow up, it appears

2   Loehr, J. & Schwartz, T. (2003). *The Power of Full Engagement: Managing Energy, not Time, is the Key to High Performance and Personal Renewal.* New York: Free Press, p. 3.

that, for many of us, a balanced life that includes an appropriate level of renewal, or play, is becoming a thing of the past because, as adults, we think we should act more responsibly. We put away our toys and favorite games to get on with our lives of working for a living, feeding our families, paying the bills, and parenting. Soon, we begin to think that play is "just for kids," and our days of joyful abandon become nothing more than a sweet memory. But for those of us with dogs, we have a constant reminder that play is a wondrous way to reconnect with the puppy inside of us, too!

DOGS AT PLAY

"A Great Dane, at its shoulders the height of a small horse, spots his target across the lawn: a 6-pound Chihuahua almost hidden in the high grass. With one languorous leap, his ears perked, the Dane arrives in front of the trembling Chihuahua. He lowers his head and bows to the little dog, raising his rear end up in the air and wagging his tail. Instead of fleeing, the Chihuahua mirrors this pose in return and leaps onto the head of the Dane, embracing his nose with her tiny paws. They begin to play."[3]

This moving description of the ritual behaviors that dogs display to communicate their desire to play was written by Dr. Alexandra Horowitz, Director of the Horowitz Dog Cognition Lab at Barnard College in New York City. It is easy to picture the apprehension that the tiny Chihuahua must have felt at the approach of the enormous Great Dane. Imagine how you would react if a full-grown bull elephant approached you, indicating in some way that it wanted to play, and you, recognizing the intention, leapt onto its trunk with the sense of security that you would not be squashed like a pancake.[4]

---

3   Retrieved June 10, 2015, from http://insideofadog.com/

4   Horowitz, A. (2004). Dog Minds and Dog Play. (Draft copy). From M. Bekoff, (ed.). *Encyclopedia of Animal Behavior.* Westport, CT: Greenwood Press, pp. 835-836.

Dogs love to play and, as with humans, this behavior arises early in their lives. One of Dr. Horowitz's colleagues at the cognition lab, Julie Hecht, observed that at about three weeks of age, puppies begin a series of behaviors, including rolling over their littermates, nipping, rearing up, and chasing each other.[5] Through these play behaviors, the puppies begin to learn and practice skills they will use throughout their lives. Researchers like Julie and Dr. Horowitz are discovering that play in puppies is a rehearsal for adult behaviors that prepare the dog for the interactions he or she will have in the years ahead. Dr. Nicholas Dodman says that in nature, dogs who have played as puppies may even have an edge over their counterparts who may be "still struggling to learn the Ps and Qs and the rudiments of the chase."[6] Dodman notes that play, by definition, is fun. I think we would all agree that dogs love to have fun!

Recall from the last chapter that dogs have clear behavioral cues they follow to communicate their intentions. When it comes to play, dogs have unique behaviors such as the play bow, in which they go down on their elbows with their rear ends elevated and their tails raised and usually wagging. In this posture, dogs generally have on their "let's play" faces, with their mouths open, tongues hanging out, and ears pricked forward. To these behaviors, they may also add barking and dancing around to signal their desire to play.

5   Hecht, J. (2012, December 12). How Do You Play With Your Dog? *Scientific American*. Retrieved from http://blogs.
     scientificamerican.com/guest-blog/how-do-you-play-with-your-dog/
6   Dodman, D. (2014, September 21). How Dogs Play. Retrieved from www.petplace.com/article/dogs/behavior-training/
     normal-behavior/how-dogs-play

When dogs like Panda, Skeeter, and their canine buddies play, they engage in a wide range of behaviors, including running, chasing each other, wrestling, nipping, and playing "keep-away" with toys or sticks. As parents, we liken the joy of watching two dogs romp around together with the pleasure we feel when we watch our children—oblivious to the adults around them—playing make-believe with their friends. The children get entirely caught up in their own world of enjoyment and fun, and, like the dogs, they are practicing skills, roles, and behaviors that will be helpful in the future.

Panda is always ready to play. Every opportunity to chase a ball or engage in a tug of war with a rope toy appears to be pure bliss. Garry shares that Panda will get one of his toys and bring it to Garry and his wife with the obvious expectation that they should play with him. If Garry and Lauren say "not now," Panda will drop whatever toy he brought, run back to his pile of toys, and bring another one. He will continue to bring toys until Garry and Lauren have a pile of toys at their feet and finally give in, throwing a ball or getting down on the floor with him to play tug of war. They have been through this routine enough times to know that Panda will not give up until he gets the playtime he wants—and Panda knows his family well enough to know that Garry and Lauren eventually will give in.

If you have a dog, you know that when you take him for a walk, he can find genuine interest in every leaf, stick, tree, fire hydrant, and clod of dirt you pass! Certainly, dogs have a far greater sense of smell than we do, but they get so excited and enjoy interacting with everything they see and smell that it helps us appreciate the world around us more as well.

THE BENEFITS OF PLAY

Dogs often appear to have cornered the market when it comes to understanding the value of play. Granted, dogs have simpler lives, but we can still learn a lot from them about the importance of play at a time when many people seem to think it is vital to work ten to twelve hours a day. The good news is that we can reanimate the spark of play in our lives and get back on the fast track to greater happiness and life balance through play. Garry recalls seeing a television segment with comedian Daniel Tosh in which Tosh observed that a person simply cannot be depressed on a wave runner. Tosh mimicked bouncing through the waves with a frown on his face and, after five or ten seconds, began to smile broadly. In a similar vein, comedian

Steve Martin once said, "The banjo is such a happy instrument—you just can't play a sad song on the banjo."[7] We agree with Steve because neither of us can recall ever hearing a depressing banjo tune, either; they are always upbeat and happy.

Fortunately, there are a million things we can do to have fun and engage in play in our lives besides wave runners and banjos. Let's face it: you can be sixty years old and go down a long, curvy waterslide headfirst, and you will have regressed to age ten by the time you reach the pool because something inside you has come alive again.

"Adults need to play because so much of our life is utilitarian," said University of South Alabama's Catherine O'Keefe. "We need to reconnect with the things of our lives that ground us in who we are and why we like our lives."[8] This sentiment is echoed by Stuart Brown, a professor at the Baylor College of Medicine in Houston. He interviewed more than 6,000 people about their upbringing, and his findings confirmed that play is vital for us to learn to be socially skillful, acquire cognitive skills, solve problems, and cope with stress (sounds like what puppies gain from playing, doesn't it?).

7   Retrieved March 15, 2015, from www.goodreads.com/quotes/97570-the-banjo-is-such-a-happy-instrument--you-can-t-play-a

8   Cited in The Key to Happiness: A Taboo for Adults? *Huffington Post Healthy Living*. (2011, January 18) Retrieved from www.huffingtonpost.com/joe-robinson/why-is-the-key-source-of-_b_809719.html

Professor Brown observes, "Play is often portrayed as a time when we feel most alive, yet we often take it for granted and may completely forget about it."[9] But play isn't a luxury—it's a necessity. Play is as important to our physical and mental health as getting enough sleep, eating well, and exercising. Play teaches us how to manage and transform our "negative" emotions and experiences. It supercharges learning, helps us relieve stress, and connects us to others and the world around us.

When our canine friends become playful, they do it with great pleasure, approaching every walk or game as an adventure to be embraced wholeheartedly. Dogs make sure to play every chance they get. Pick up a favorite toy, and Fido's ears perk up and he becomes a bundle of energy, ready for fun. When I merely put on my jogging shoes or reach for the leash, Panda knows I'm going outside and becomes a force of joy to be reckoned with.

Researchers define play as an activity that spurs upbeat emotions and lets people get acquainted with each other, learning about one another by connecting together in mutual play. This happens faster just by virtue of the neurological effects of play

9   Brown, S. (2009). *Play: How It Shapes the Brain, Opens the Imagination, and Invigorates the Soul.* New York: Penguin Books, p. 5.

because it infuses the interaction with laughter, smiling, and good feelings. Play encourages everyone who participates to rid themselves of aggressions, stress, and tension. It has been found that couples who play together, whether in activities or playful innuendo, report greater intimacy and closeness.[10]

Dr. Stuart Brown is the founder of The National Institute for Play, an organization devoted to unlocking human potential through play in all stages of life by using science to discover all that play has to teach us about transforming our world. Dr. Brown observes, "Play is the gateway to vitality. By its nature, it is uniquely and intrinsically rewarding. It generates optimism, seeks out novelty, makes perseverance fun, leads to mastery, gives the immune system a boost, fosters empathy, and promotes a sense of belonging and community. Each of these play by-products are indices of personal health, and their shortage predicts impending health problems and personal fragility. A life or a culture devoid of or deficient in play exists as a heightened major public health risk factor. The prevalence of depression, stress-related diseases, interpersonal violence, the addictions, and other health and well-being problems can be linked, like a deficiency disease, to

10   Gordon, G. Retrieved May 15, 2015, from www.gwengordonplay.com/pdf/what_is_play.pdf

the prolonged deprivation of play. Each person has a unique play personality...
when one remains in touch with it...when it is actualized, it empowers and brings
pleasure to life."[11]

PLAY AT WORK

It's only 10 a.m., and it seems the workday will never end. The hands on the clock
seem to be stuck, and the work in your inbox continues to pile up. You feel brain-
dead, and your body revolts from the stress and boredom of the workday.

For many people, the foregoing paragraph describes every day at work. Many,
if not most, of us are under the impression that if we just work harder and longer
every day, then our workload will go away. Wrong. There is always more to do. Do
you work for a company that is always asking you to do more with less? Despite
our best efforts, we feel as though we are falling behind, becoming chronically
overwhelmed and burning out.

This is unfortunate because work is where we spend a great deal of our time—
usually eight to ten hours a day, five days a week. This is why it is especially
important for us to enjoy what we do and find time to play during work. Without
some sense of fun and recreation, work becomes...well, work. And who wants

11   Personal Health and Well Being. Carmel Valley, CA: The National Institute for Play. Retrieved May 13, 2015, from www.
      nifplay.org/opportunities/personal-health/

that? Success at work does not depend on the amount of time you work; it depends on the quality of the work you do. And the quality of the work you do is highly dependent on your sense of joy, well-being, and accomplishment.

Taking time to replenish yourself through play is one of the best things you can do for your career. When a project you are working on hits a serious stumbling block, as it often will, it presents you with a great opportunity to take a break, do something fun, or have a few laughs with a colleague to take your mind off the problem.

We have consistently found that encouraging play and entertaining activities at work is a great way to spur creativity and build positive relationships. Play and engagement help keep us from being too narrowly focused on one path or one goal. For example, I notice that when I go out for a walk with Panda, it is easy for me to fall into the mindset of viewing the walk as simply navigating from Point A (our house) to Point B (the park) and back. My goal is to accomplish "the walk" as quickly and efficiently as possible and to remain on the sidewalk. I can assure you that Panda has never shared this perspective.

For Panda, a walk to the park is an indeterminate, winding, chaotic meandering that has nothing to do with staying on the sidewalk and has everything to do with

investigating every little leaf, twig, scrap of paper or any other object he can see or smell. He is constantly alert for and interested in anything new or different. And because Panda is truly exploring and vigilant during each and every walk, I am forced to pay attention to everything he discovers. In fact, if we simply conducted the walk as I had originally envisioned, it would soon become dull and routine— not fun at all. Instead, each outing becomes an adventure for me as well because I am constantly surprised at what Panda finds along the way.

At work, we often get into mundane routines as well. One of the most common complaints among managers and employees is the boring meetings they must attend. If you want to have a near-death experience, attend a meeting of academic administrators. Keep in mind that our educational philosophy and curriculum are predicated on teaching the cutting edge in creativity, passion, and employee engagement. Yet almost every meeting is conducted with the same level of somber routine. Everyone files in, each person takes his or her place at the same spot (generally based on hierarchy, with the most senior sitting closest to the highest ranking administrator, and the rest lined up in descending order), and then, when asked, each provides an update with a lack of zeal that would induce a zombie to keel over. Regardless of where you work, how many times have you had to suffer through meetings like this?

Personal Activity:

PLAY AT WORK

Take a minute to think about the meetings you normally attend. How often have you had to attend a poorly planned and/or conducted meeting?

_____

What was it like to have to sit through the meeting?

_____

What could have been done to make the meeting more fun and productive?

More companies are realizing that employee attitudes about their work, their performance, and their creativity are greatly enhanced by incorporating play into the workplace. Shifting the business model toward mixing fun and work can rejuvenate the work environment, keep stress at bay, and encourage job contentment. Employees become more positive, cooperative, and social, and they will achieve more when given difficult tasks. Studies have shown that the far-reaching, affirmative effects of play last up to twenty-four hours, keeping the mind active and lighthearted afterward.[12]

12   The Benefits of Play for Adults: How Play Can Improve Your Health, Work and Family Relationships. Retrieved January 12, 2014, from www.helpguide.org/articles/emotional-health/benefits-of-play-for-adults.htm

Several companies have great reputations for not only being fun places at which to work but also for being highly profitable and productive. Southwest Airlines has consistently been named one of America's top-five most admired companies in *Fortune* magazine's annual poll. It also receives high marks in customer service while achieving higher levels of quality and profitability than its competitors. Perhaps some of the reason is that play is part of Southwest's way of life.

Southwest employees work hard and intentionally incorporate fun into their daily operations. The late Herb Kelleher, founder of Southwest Airlines, was renowned for dressing up in costumes, holding pep-rally meetings, and joking with passengers and employees alike. During his tenure as CEO of Southwest, Kelleher's colorful personality created a corporate culture that made Southwest employees well known for taking themselves lightly—often singing in-flight announcements to the tune of popular theme songs—but taking their jobs seriously.

Garry recalls an associate, Tim Kight, President of Focus 3 Consulting, relating a conversation he'd had with a Southwest Airlines flight attendant. Tim asked the flight attendant if she liked working for the airline. "Oh, yes! I love it!" she exclaimed. He then asked if she knew flight attendants from competitor airlines and if they would like to work for Southwest. "Yes, flight crews often ride shuttles to and from hotels together, so we get to know each other pretty well. Most of my colleagues at other airlines would quit in a minute to come to Southwest," she replied. Tim then asked her the most significant question: would she recommend

them as potential employees? "Oh, no," she responded emphatically. "They are much too serious and just wouldn't fit with our culture!"[13]

Ben and Jerry's Ice Cream is another company that has figured out that having fun at work is great for everyone. Ben and Jerry's has a permanent employee committee called the Joy Gang. This committee has the enviable job of planning fun activities for employees by (1) making Joy Grants of up to $500 for fun ideas that will create joy in the workplace (a hot cocoa machine for the freezer crew, a stereo for the production crew, and so on), (2) creating permanent spontaneity through regular outlandish surprises, and (3) creating planned contests and events, such as "Clash Dressing Day," holiday gift exchanges, and "Celebrate Chocolate Week."[14]

Google employees are paid to play beach volleyball, go bowling, or scale a climbing wall, activities that take place at the search engine company's main campus in California. At LinkedIn, employees can play foosball or Ping-Pong when they tire of emails. And many of you may be familiar with the famous Pike Place Fish Market in Seattle. The employees at Pike Place Fish Market draw huge crowds who gawk at them throwing fish to each other, joking with customers, and asking passersby to help perform CPR on dead fish. It is an atmosphere that keeps everyone energized and having fun.[15]

13   Interview with Tim Knight, SHRM Student Regional Conference, April 29, 2014.
14   Deal, T. (1998). Corporate Celebration: Play, Purpose and Profit at Work. San Francisco, CA: Berrett Koehler Publisher, p. 109.
15   Ibid.

Of course, we can't forget the value that dogs bring to the workplace. Companies such as Purina, Amazon, and the software firm Inverse-Square have found that allowing employees to bring pets to work is beneficial. According to a study published in the *International Journal of Workplace Health Management*, the presence of dogs in the workplace significantly lowered the staff members' stress throughout the day.[16] In fact, many companies with reputations for being great places to work are dog friendly. One of the key benefits of dogs is their ability to break down the barriers that keep humans from connecting. After all, how many times have you chatted easily with a stranger while petting his or her dog? When dogs are around, many people feel relaxed and happy. Just the other night, Sharon said she came home from work at 10:00 p.m., walked to the mailbox by the street, and met two ladies and their dogs out for a stroll. They exchanged talk about the dogs' names and habits and chatted easily for ten minutes or so. Everyone was relaxed and happy to "talk dog."

FAMILY AND PERSONAL PLAY

Some of our sweetest memories come from childhood play—board games, tree climbing, hide-and-seek, kick the can, playing house, street football, and the list goes on. It was through play that we learned to be responsible, and play is the foundation of a healthy, happy child.

16   Abraham, S. (2012, March 30). Benefits of Taking Fido to Work May Not be Far-Fetched. *VCU News*. Retrieved from www.news.vcu.edu/article/

Great things also happen when families play together. You have surely heard the saying "the family that plays together, stays together" (or something like that). Having fun together is a crucial characteristic of happy, healthy families. Our children certainly need to go to school and do their chores, and they need appropriate care, but what they need just as much is the opportunity to engage with their parents in an exciting game of tag, Monopoly, or kickball or to go with their parents to the swimming pool or on a nature walk. Families make memories and share inside jokes, work stress melts away, and bonds become stronger. For many families, good old-fashioned play is the glue that keeps it all together.

But, somewhere along the line, we either forgot how to play or simply found ourselves overwhelmed by the demands of busy lives. We became adults with huge responsibilities, such as families to provide for, house payments to make, career ladders to climb—it never stops. We are reluctant to play because we are afraid we will look silly. It is no wonder we are a stressed-out, worn-out population. And, for some reason, society views adult play as being irresponsible because there are a million more constructive things to accomplish.

Our canine friends are experts when it comes to play. They seem to naturally perceive that fun is important, and dogs don't care how we look. What happens when you pick up your dog's favorite toy? How does he react to the squeak he hears from that toy? His ears perk up, his eyes brighten, he is on full alert, and he is ready to play! A dog's desire to play is a barometer of his health and well-being. It is no different for you and your family. Consider these correlations between child play and dog play.

Children play pretend to discover their roles in the world, to try out adult behaviors, and to hone social skills, which are the same reasons puppies play shortly after birth. Kids love to play ball games, run, chase, and jump, all the while strengthening their physical health. Puppies play to strengthen their bones and muscles even though they don't realize it.

Playing with other children is very important for a child to learn about roles in life, how to get along with others, and social skills. Dogs who play with other dogs grow up healthier and better adjusted, too.

Southwest Airlines, Ben and Jerry's Ice Cream, Google, LinkedIn, and the Pike Place Fish Market are just a few of the companies that have realized that play in the workplace pays off big. The idea that a joyful working space creates healthy benefits for employees is catching on. One of the best cases for ensuring greater fun on the job comes from the Great Place to Work Institute. At the companies ranked by the institute as being among the Top 100 Great Places to Work, employees responded overwhelmingly that they work in a fun environment. Amy Lyman, cofounder of the institute, says that it would be very unusual for a company to be on the list of the top 100 companies and not earn a high score for being a fun workplace. Research on these and other top companies makes it very clear that if people are having fun, they work harder, stay longer, and maintain their composure better during times of stress. Plus, employees who are having fun are also more innovative and creative; they solve problems and work more effectively with others.

Just take it from the dog—play is important for good mental, emotional, and physical health. We need to look closely at our canine friends to understand that play is vital to our well-being in all aspects of life. Society could benefit greatly if we could learn how to play again as adults. Having fun brings an endless list of benefits that will make us better people, parents, employers, employees, and family members. Just look at our four-legged furry friends, who never forget how to play and who enjoy life no matter how old they are.

Wag more and bark less.

Thinking about Play

Do you remember how to play? In the space below, make a list of the things you remember enjoying the most when you were a child. What were the activities in which you found the greatest joy? When were you able to really let yourself go?

Based on your answers to the previous question, do you see any patterns? Were these activities in which you played alone, or did you include others? Were the activities thoughtful or energetic? Did you play mostly indoors or outdoors? What are the common themes?

Keep track of what you enjoy most now. As you go through your busy week, keep a notebook handy where you can jot down all the things you enjoy. What causes you to laugh, to smile, and to engage with others in a positive way? Make a commitment to look for opportunities to engage in these activities more often.

Do you have a hobby or something to occupy you in your free time, or do you find yourself stuck in front of the television for hours on end? Explore a hobby that you find interesting and engaging: woodworking, bird watching, stamp collecting, dancing, art, writing, cartooning, sculpting, brewing beer, hiking…there are many options. You don't have to be great at it, and you don't have to stay with it if you find it's not what you had in mind.

CHAPTER 4

UNCONDITIONAL LOVE

The one absolutely unselfish friend that a man can have in this selfish world, the one that never deserts him, and the one that never proves ungrateful or treacherous is his dog. He will kiss the hand that has no food to offer, he will lick the wounds and sores that come in encounters with the roughness of the world. He guards the sleep of his pauper master as if he were a prince. When all other friends desert, he remains. When riches take the wings and reputation falls to pieces, he is as constant in his love as the sun in its journey through the heaven.

—GEORGE GRAHAM VEST
(C. 1855)

*F*ew who have lived with dogs would deny that dogs have emotions. When I observe Panda, his emotions are evident in the sincere joy he displays when we go for walks in the local park. When I let him off leash, he gallops ahead and through the underbrush in what appears to be a state of delight. While he is quite brave in some respects, he is also clearly terrified of the vacuum cleaner. When we vacuum the house, he hides on top of the bed, trembling, with a look of anxiety. If he thinks we are going for a walk, but I am simply getting my coat to go to the store, he shuffles back to the living room and drops down in disappointment. And, there are those times when our family is sitting around, watching a movie, and Panda is lying with his head in my son's lap. The look on his face and his body posture convey a picture of absolute contentment and calm.

When we speak with groups, those in the audience frequently identify a dog's unconditional love for its family members as one of the qualities they appreciate most. But not everyone feels this way. Skeptics argue that dogs are not capable of love and, at best, do not feel emotions like humans do. These doubters argue that dogs are simply acting out of their own self-interest and are manipulating us by behaving in ways that benefit them. To the contrary, my experience, that of millions of dog owners, and recent research indicate that dogs are both fully capable of and do feel emotions much as we do. Reflect on the earlier story of Bella, who ran to fight off the coyote to save her best little friend from death. That story destroys the "no emotions" and "only self-

interest" arguments quickly. Consider the following story told by Stanley Coren in *Modern Dog* magazine.[1]

DOG LOVE

Rocky, a 65-pound Boxer, and Rita, a shy eleven-year-old girl, lived in the Finger Lakes region of New York State. Rita got Rocky when he was just ten weeks old, and they quickly became inseparable. Rita took great pride in feeding and grooming Rocky, and he slept on her bed at night. When Rita was not in school, the two spent so much time together that her family referred to the two as "R and R."

The only time the two were not together was when Rita would go swimming. As a puppy, Rocky had lived with a family who had a young boy with emotional problems. On two occasions, the boy's father had to rescue the puppy from being drowned by the little boy. After the second incident, the father returned Rocky to the breeder for Rocky's own safety. As a result of these early ordeals, water was the only thing Rocky truly feared. When Rita would go swimming, Rocky would watch her intently, running along the shore and whimpering until she returned. But he would not go into the water at all.

One day, after Rocky had been in Rita's family for several years, Rita's mother

1   Coen, S. (2007). Can Dogs Love? *Modern Dog Magazine*. Retrieved May 13, 2015, from http://Moderndogmagazine.com/articles/can-dogs-love-true-story/132

took the two of them to a shopping area located next to a lake with a wooden boardwalk along the shore. Next to the boardwalk was an embankment that dropped steeply more than 20 feet down to the surface of the water. As Rita's mother shopped some distance away, Rita and Rocky were playing on the boardwalk. All of a sudden, a boy on a bicycle came riding down the boardwalk

and slammed on his brakes, skidding on the damp surface and crashing into Rita at an angle. The force of the blow drove her through the boardwalk's guardrail and into the water far below. Rita hit the water hard and lay face down and unmoving.

Rocky, the dog who refused to set even a paw in the water, looked down, saw Rita floating in the water, and leaped through the same opening Rita had fallen through, into the water below. He swam quickly to Rita and grabbed her by the shoulder strap of her dress, which fortunately caused her to roll face-up. Rocky then pulled her to shore and stood beside her, licking her face and whining until rescuers were able to make it down the steep embankment. If it had not been for Rocky, Rita would almost certainly have drowned.

It is interesting to note that following this incident, Rocky's fear of the water never diminished. Rocky continued to avoid water for the rest of his life.

What compels a dog who is terrified of water to leap in to save his best friend's life? Rocky was certainly not acting out of self-interest, and he even risked his own life in taking action to save Rita. As Stanley Coren so aptly concluded this story, "No one, at least not Rita or her family, ever doubted his love for her. [Rocky] lived long enough to see an event occur [that] would not have happened had he not cared for her as much as he did. When Rita graduated from high school, she posed for a photo in her cap and gown. Beside her sat a now much older Boxer. The smiling girl

had an arm around the dog, and her hand was cinched in his collar, [just] as it was the day [when] Rocky unambiguously showed her just how much he loved her."[2]

FINDING THE RIGHT GUY

Consider a similar story about what we can learn from the unconditional love of a dog. Kathleen is a striking, vivacious woman who works as an executive assistant at a high-tech company. Following her divorce, Kathleen adopted Noel, a female black Labrador Retriever. Noel had been abused and, as a result, was shy and took some time to warm up to new people.[3] The rescue organization would allow families to "try her out" for a few days, but because she was slow to bond, especially with men, she was always returned. However, when Kathleen took Noel home, she knew that Noel would be hers for life.

Kathleen learned over the years that Noel does offer unconditional love to those who have patience. When Noel meets a new person, Kathleen tells him or her to simply leave Noel alone and to let the dog approach on her terms. Kathleen observed, "I believe I have learned a lot from Noel about not pushing myself or others into relationships. Trust needs to be built with her just like with a human

2   *Ibid.*
3   Interview conducted on September 12, 2012.

being. As a single mom with two teenage sons, it is easy for me to want to rush a dating relationship with someone else; sometimes, the person I am dating wants to rush the relationship with me. That has always turned out to be a bad idea." She went on to explain, "Being with Noel constantly reminds me that you can't rush true love, but once it is earned, you will have it forever."

While Noel may be timid, Kathleen has also found that her dog has great intuition about people. "I have actually used Noel as a litmus test of sorts. As a single woman out in the dating world, I've found her to be a great judge of character. (We actually think this is true for all dogs in general!) I always explain to potential dates about her shyness, and I have been amazed at how some would react. One man, who said he was a dog lover, apparently was very strict with how he expected a dog to behave. He walked in my house and, instead of ignoring her when she barked, he starting clapping at her and only scared her more. He told me she shouldn't act that way and didn't even appreciate her sniffing him once she did settle down." Kathleen paused and then went on, "His actions made several important things very clear. First, he didn't listen to me when I explained her situation. Second, [because] he felt he could so brazenly tell me how to raise my dog, I suspect he would most likely do the same thing in regard to my children, and it was not his place to do so." Kathleen laughed. "Needless to say, I didn't see him again!"

She went on to say, "On the other hand, I've had dates who have gone out of their way to make friends with her, and that meant a lot to me. I don't feed her 'people food,' but one guy would give her a little of the fat off his steak. He was showing me that he was willing to share with my dog, and he wanted her to trust him. I didn't scold him for giving her food because the intent behind the action was more important. Over the years, I've actually worried more about how a date would interact with Noel than how they would interact with my kids! If they couldn't make friends with her, they never got to meet my children."

I asked Kathleen how she made sense of the amazing love Noel showed her and her children. She said, "When I see how Noel looks at me, it is clear that my kids and I are everything to her. She is so accepting of who we are. She does not appear to see our shortcomings and just thinks we are perfect." Kathleen wisely added, "We, on the other hand, are acutely aware of and beat ourselves up for our shortcomings. Dogs don't do that. They accept themselves the way they are, and they accept and love us just as we are. I think our lives would be better if we learned to be that way."

UNDERSTANDING LOVE

Love is a phenomenon that human beings and scientists have been trying to figure out forever; perhaps it is the mystery and intensity of love that makes this emotion so intriguing. The power of love has been illustrated for thousands of years by human beings through poetry, music, novels, stage productions, television shows, and movies. Human beings live for and will sacrifice themselves for love, and science has found that there is a very good reason.

Scientific research has shed some light on the nature of love. Experiments conducted on the brain using magnetic resonance imaging (MRI) show that the "feel-good" sensation of romance is generated by dopamine, a neurotransmitter that helps control the brain's reward and pleasure centers. Dopamine also helps regulate movement and emotional responses, and it enables us not only to see rewards but also to take action to move toward them. When you look forward to a date with someone special, a big party, a winning hand in cards, or getting a big raise, it is the flow of dopamine that makes the feeling such a pleasure.[4]

---

4   Retrieved June 10, 2015, from www.brainhq.com/brain-resources/brain-facts-myths/brain-in-love

But dopamine by itself does not equal love. Think of it this way: You may go out with someone once or twice and have a good time but never go out again. And even if you win at a slot machine or attend a great party, you will eventually tire of the event and walk away. Something else has to happen—something that goes beyond just a feeling of pleasure—to turn the thrill of a relationship with someone else into an obsession. That substance is called oxytocin, and it is the chemical that helps people form long-term emotional bonds with each other as well as fostering trust and compassion. People who are in love experience elevated levels of oxytocin. Not surprisingly, oxytocin is also produced through gentle touch and caressing, such as that which occurs when we pet or stroke dogs. This action and the resulting emotions are associated with the bonding between human beings and our animals.[5]

Utilizing MRI technology, scientists have been able to confirm that dogs also produce oxytocin. As social animals, dogs share an evolutionary need for forming close emotional ties with others. Dr. Bruce Fogel, a veterinarian, explains that over thousands of years, dogs have evolved the same capacity for vulnerability, dependence, and love that we humans experience.[6] Like humans,

5   Retrieved May 30, 2016, from http://well.blogs.nytimes.com/2015/04/16/the-look-of-love-is-in-the-dogs-eyes/?_r=0
6   Retrieved July 21, 2015, from www.dailymail.co.uk/news/article-2094157/Why-dog-really-DOES-love-just-treats-it.html

dogs are gregarious social creatures, and their ability to love helps us live together productively, work in harmony, and build strong relationships. So it is not simply the imagination of dog owners that their dogs have the capacity for love; dogs have the very same chemical mechanisms as humans for forming loving relationships.

This brings us to three deeper questions. First, what do we mean when we use the term "unconditional" love? Second, what does it mean to say that dogs demonstrate this unconditional love? Third, how can we human beings demonstrate healthy unconditional love more effectively?

WHAT IS UNCONDITIONAL LOVE?

Let's begin by considering if there is such a thing as unconditional love. When people picture unconditional love, they imagine love that has no boundaries, limits, or reason. We picture this kind of love as one that will stay exactly the way it is regardless of any circumstances or conditions within the relationship and whether it is returned or not. Generally, we apply this term to family members or when we consider our spiritual beliefs. Most people's parents and siblings will always be there even if the family disagrees, and the basic love and lasting bond will always exist. Spouses ideally marry for life and "for better or worse." For those with strong spiritual beliefs, we also say that God loves us unconditionally.

Dr. Jeremy Nicholson, a doctor of social and personality psychology, wrote in *Psychology Today* that while it is possible for human beings to love unconditionally, it is also important to recognize that healthy relationships also have limits. Individuals may love one another unconditionally but also set boundaries and clarify expectations to ensure that a balanced, healthy relationship exists.

Dr. Nicholson stresses that while we can "feel" love unconditionally, we may choose to end an unhealthy relationship when the conditions for maintaining that relationship are no longer healthy or sensible. For example, if a relationship becomes one in which one of the people is saying, "You may treat me horribly and you can do anything to me, and I will ignore my needs and be true to you," that is a loss of authentic self and an unhealthy relationship.[7] Other examples of destructive relationships include those that are physically, mentally, and/or sexually abusive, or those in which someone has become an enabler of the other's negative behavior (drugs, alcohol, gambling, and so on.)

In her book, *Fight Less, Love More: 5-Minute Conversations to Change Your Relationship without Blowing Up or Giving In*, Laurie Puhn says that in order for mature love to

7   Nicholson, J. (2011). Do You Believe in Unconditional Love? *Psychology Today*. Retrieved from www.psychologytoday.com/blog/the-attraction-doctor/201107/do-you-believe-in-unconditional-love

HOW DO YOU DEMONSTRATE LOVE?

We all like to be loved, but have you really taken time to think about love in your life? In the space below, describe how you believe you demonstrate your love to others.

Now, describe what others do or can do that make you feel loved.

Are there differences between how you demonstrate love to others and how you like others to demonstrate love to you?

survive and thrive, those in the relationship must show genuine appreciation, respect, compassion, trust, and companionship. She points out that if any of those qualities is "compromised by lies, neglect, rudeness, unnecessary criticism, stubbornness, or secrets…then the love is no longer grounded."[8]

Laurie's message is that in healthy, loving relationships, partners have enough self-respect to set limits and recognize that if lines are crossed, there will be negative consequences. Parents love their children unconditionally, but they also expect their kids to meet certain standards of behavior and conform to certain norms. Spouses understand that to sustain a healthy, growing relationship, both partners must demonstrate respect, trust, and fidelity to each other. In healthy relationships, there may be disagreements over where to go on vacation, how to spend money, or whether to buy this car or that one, but the love endures.

---

8   As cited in Neumann. (2011). Is Unconditional Love Unhealthy? Retrieved from www.match.com/magazine/article/12019/

HOW DO DOGS DEMONSTRATE LOVE?

Now that we know what we mean by the term "unconditional love," let's look at the second question; how do dogs demonstrate unconditional love? As noted earlier, dogs have the biological capability and clearly demonstrate a range of other emotions including love. One of the more obvious manifestations of a dog's unconditional love is that dogs are so amazingly accepting of us. It does not matter to a dog if you are fat, skinny, young, old, ill, disabled, tall, or short. Dogs don't care one bit about sexual preference, religion, race, nationality, or gender. They love you no matter what. For human beings, all of these qualities are of great importance. People discriminate, oppress, denigrate, and even kill over religion, race, and gender bias in our culture.

Dogs also bond with humans and have done so for thousands of years. They are consistently happy and even excited to be with us. As we have mentioned, every time we come home from work or when the kids return from school, our dogs are absolutely thrilled to see us as they dance around and wag their rear ends enthusiastically. Garry tells the story about needing to go to the store one day, but as he backed down the driveway, he remembered he had forgotten the shopping list in the kitchen. He pulled back in and stepped in the doorway, and by Panda's energetic greeting, you would have thought he had been gone for a year. How many of your friends are that excited to see you?

Another way dogs demonstrate their love is by always being interested in doing just about anything we want to do. Want to go for a walk? So does Fido. Want to sing and dance around the room? So does Fifi. Want to throw the ball, sit quietly, or watch television? Chances are pretty good that your dog will be thrilled to engage in that activity too.

Dogs are also very protective. Our dogs have always taken their responsibility to keep our home and children safe seriously. When someone rings the doorbell, your dog is quickly there, barking a warning. If a big truck goes rumbling down the street, your dog dashes to the window to make sure the premises are safe. Years ago, when Garry's children were just toddlers, they were fascinated by the swimming pool or any body of water. At the time, Garry and his wife had two wonderful Springer Spaniels, Spot and Domino, who took particular pride in watching out for the children. Spot and Domino would walk back and forth between the toddlers and the swimming pool to keep them from getting too close and falling in accidentally. They did this with such regularity that it was clearly a protective action on their part. They did not behave this way when the kids were playing in other settings or when an adult approached the pool.

Dogs also have an amazing ability to forgive. They do not harbor grudges as do we humans. You can be a complete grouch, ignore your dog, or talk harshly to him,

but he still loves you. And, like good lovers, the more love and attention you give them, the more they give you in return. The relationship simply grows stronger and stronger, day after day.

What really amazes humans is that a dog's love for us is not self-centered, scheming, or manipulative. A dog's heart, as my poetic Belarusian friend Andrei said, is like the purest crystal. There is no deceit, treachery, or dishonesty. However, in alignment with what we have seen is true about unconditional love, there are limits. That a dog demonstrates an encompassing love for us does not mean that he is perfect and never misbehaves. It also does not mean that he is not possessive of certain belongings or his food. For example, if Panda is eating, Garry can reach down and take the food bowl or a dog bone right out of his mouth. One of his previous Springer Spaniels, on the other hand, would snarl a warning and snap if a family member tried to take his food.

DEMONSTRATING UNCONDITIONAL LOVE MORE EFFECTIVELY

The third question is how can human beings demonstrate unconditional love more effectively? I think Laurie Puhn is on target when she states that true love is characterized through genuine appreciation, respect, compassion, trust, and companionship. In *How to Win Friends and Influence People*, author Dale Carnegie says that one of the best ways to get along well with others and build strong relationships is to show sincere appreciation for their efforts.[9] This principle has been proved true in my life again and again because people are eager to go above and beyond the norm when what they do is recognized. They tend to stop being motivated when their actions and efforts are ignored.

Human beings and dogs like to be appreciated because we all want to be a part of something greater than we are. We pursue professions in which we feel a sense of accomplishment and can establish relationships with others where we can work together to achieve value in our lives and the lives of others. When one person

---

9   Carnegie, D. (2005) *How to Win Friends and Influence People*. London: Cornerstone Publishing.

genuinely recognizes the efforts of another, it validates them as human beings and provides motivation for them to continue that behavior or action. When you do not demonstrate appreciation, you are implying that the other person and his or her efforts are not important to you. When someone consistently receives a message that his or her efforts are not appreciated, he or she begins to interpret this to mean that he or she is not of value either.

So when should you show appreciation? Well, keep in mind that the goal is to show genuine appreciation; a fake show of appreciation is very hollow and may even be interpreted by another person as validation that he or she is unimportant. To show true appreciation, ignore the things that you do not appreciate and recognize those actions or behaviors that you do appreciate. So, for example, if someone at work does something that demonstrates excellent service or offers to help another employee, tell him or her how much you appreciate his or her efforts. Sometimes, letting the person's supervisor know that you are pleased is appropriate. Showing appreciation does not mean that you have to give a bouquet of flowers or a monetary reward. Simply saying "thank you" and recognizing what the person did is plenty.

Recall that, in Chapter 2, Garry shared that one of his favorite ways of expressing gratitude at work is to buy one of those pizza-sized chocolate chip cookies, have "Thanks a Million!" written on it in icing, and then personally deliver it to the individual or work unit. People always appreciate the recognition, and the huge cookie is a hit with Garry's coworkers.

For those of you who have a hard time thinking of ways to show appreciation, a great resource is a book by Bob Nelson, *1501 Ways to Reward Employees*.[10] The book is filled with helpful, practical suggestions submitted by real employees, describing hundreds of ways (monetary and otherwise) to show appreciation and reward excellence. To put it simply, showing appreciation to those who deserve it costs you so little, and it might mean the world to the other person.[11]

The second quality of unconditional love is respect. It must be important, because R&B great Aretha Franklin sang about it, and the comedian Rodney Dangerfield frequently claimed, "I don't get no respect!"[12] So what is this thing called "respect" that we all seek? *Merriam-Webster* defines different elements of respect.[13] First, respect demonstrates esteem for or a sense of the worth or excellence of another person. For example, we demonstrate respect for our spouses when we acknowledge that we truly value their judgment and opinion. To respect also means to show a regard for your or someone else's rights, values, or beliefs. This relates to recognizing the personal core

10   Nelson, B. (2012). *1501 Ways to Reward Employees*. New York: Workman Publishing.

11   Lucas, R. L. (2016). *231 Ways to Say I Love You...and Mean It*. Casselberry, FL: Success Skills Press.

12   Visit Rodney Dangerfield's Website at www.rodney.com for a sampling of his jokes and quotes.

13   Retrieved June 5, 2015, from www.merriam-webster.com/dictionary/respect

values in another person; it does not mean that you have to agree with him or her. For example, you can respect another person's political, social, or religious views without sharing that person's particular beliefs.

There are a number of steps you can take to ensure that you are being respectful of others at home and at work. The first step in showing respect is having an open mind. By not making assumptions, we allow ourselves to consider new ways of thinking and recognize new opportunities. In the academic field, we call this being a critical thinker.[14] By being open to new ideas, you can discover new attributes or insights that may be worthy of our esteem (or respect).

You can also show respect simply by listening attentively to what others have to say. This means allowing the other person to complete his or her thoughts and not chiming in to add your own opinions. Paying attention also means making eye contact and periodically summarizing what you think the other person has said. Eye contact and checking for understanding conveys that you find what that person is saying important, and you are providing him or her the latitude to state his or her position clearly, without interruption.

Another means of showing respect is keeping your promises. When making a commitment to someone, follow through. For example, be on time; this demonstrates that you are mindful of the other person's time and validating how important he or she is to you. You are probably very familiar with the old saying "actions speak louder than words."[15]

For those of you who are parents or in a position of authority within your organization, being respectful also means being fair in the application of policies and discipline and allowing everyone to have a say. When in a position of power, being fair engenders a spirit of trust and openness that will permit the best ideas to bubble to the surface. It also gives people the feeling of security to state their point of view.

14   Retrieved June 5, 2015, from http://dictionary.reference.com/browse/Critical+thinking

15   Retrieved June 5, 2015, from http://idioms.thefreedictionary.com/Actions+speak+louder+than+words

Finally, you can show respect by ensuring that you preserve dignity both for yourself and for others and ensure that you find ways to help both parties save face. If you feel wronged, don't escalate the war. Seek ways to come to an agreement without reducing the situation to a mud-slinging contest.

The next quality of unconditional love is that of compassion. The Dalai Lama has stressed the importance of compassion, saying, "Compassion is not religious business, it is human business; it is not a luxury, it is essential for our own peace and mental stability; it is essential for human survival."[16]

You might ask why compassion is essential for human survival. The answer is that we all experience ups and downs in life. Regardless of who you are, at some point in life, your health, financial resources, employment, relationships, or some other aspect is likely going to suffer. If these challenges are not affecting you personally, then they are certainly going to be affecting others in your community.

The word *compassion* is derived from two words: "co," meaning together and "passion," meaning "a very strong feeling." That is what compassion is: the ability to see someone else in pain or distress, to feel that pain ourselves, and to strive to help lessen or eliminate that pain or discomfort.[17] It is summed up in the Golden Rule: do unto others as you would have them do unto you.[18] We are compassionate when we genuinely attempt to feel the pain, sorrow, struggles, or fears of another person and do what we can to alleviate that suffering.

Many people wonder how they can show compassion. First, simply show empathy for others. We have all experienced a great range of emotions, and to show empathy is to let the other person know that you understand his or her feelings.

---

16   Retrieved June 5, 2015, from www.dalailamaquotes.org/compassion-is-not-religious-business-it-is-human-business-it-is-not-luxury-it-is-essential-for-our-own-peace-and-mental-stability-it-is-essential-for-human-survival/

17   Retrieved June 5, 2015, from www.merriam-webster.com/dictionary/compassion

18   Retrieved June 5, 2015, from www.merriam-webster.com/dictionary/golden%20rule

For example, one day Garry's daughter came home from school and said that she had not done well on one of her exams. A sympathetic response would be for Garry to say, "Oh, that's too bad. I am sure you will do better next time." An empathetic response would be, "Sweetheart, I am sorry to hear that. You must feel terrible to have studied so hard and still not have done well on the test." In this latter response, Garry puts himself in her shoes and conveys that he understands how she must feel at doing poorly on the test.

Tim, a very successful sales manager for the Embassy Suites Hotel in Columbus, Ohio, shared the following story about how dogs can show empathy. Tim said, "One night, I was watching the news with my wife Nancy, when we learned of the Boston Marathon bombing. I just started crying softly at the senselessness of it all, and Coco, our Lab mix, came up and put her nose on my hand. She made a soft noise as if she knew something was wrong and wanted to make me feel better." As Tim's story suggests, dogs can teach us a lot about simply being aware of others' emotions and that just being present is often all we need to do to show empathy toward someone else.

We can be compassionate to ourselves as well. We might have burned something in the oven, forgotten to pick something up from the store on the way home, not called someone when we said we would, and so on. In these types of situations, we can give ourselves the benefit of the doubt instead of beating ourselves up. Being compassionate toward ourselves is recognizing that we are human, too. And the more we can have compassion for ourselves, the more we can have compassion for others.

A MODEL OF TRUST

One of the most important aspects of any loving relationship is trust. When a high level of trust exists, everything in a relationship is easier. When trust is missing, everything is in jeopardy. In his 1993 dissertation, "A Construct of Trust," Dr. Duane Tway, a professor at Walden University and president of the Trust Building Institute, observed, "There exists today no practical construct of trust that allows us to design and implement organizational interventions to significantly increase trust levels between people. We all think we know what trust is from our own experiences, but we don't know much about how to improve it. Why? I believe it is because we have been taught to look at trust as if it were a single entity."[19]

---

19   Cited in Heathfield, Susan. (2015). Trust Rules, The Most Important Secret About Trust, About Money. Retrieved May 13, 2015, from http://humanresources.about.com/od/workrelationships/a/trust_rules.htm

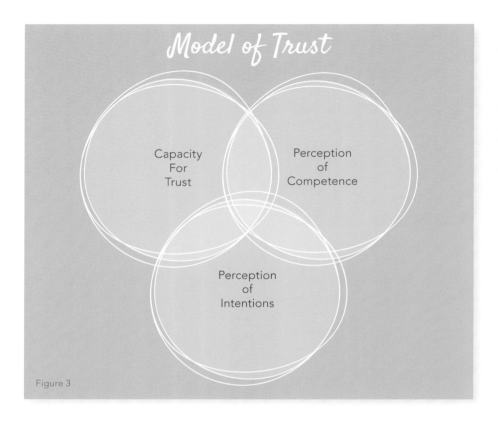

Figure 3

Dr. Tway identifies trust as "the state of readiness for unguarded interaction with someone or something." He developed a model of trust that includes three components: the capacity for trusting, the perception of competence, and the perception of intentions.[20] If you consider trust as comprising these three components, it makes trust easier to understand.

As depicted in Figure 3, the first of the three components is the capacity for trust. The capacity for trust means that all of your life experiences have developed your current willingness to risk being vulnerable to others. Some peoples' lives have made it very easy for them to trust, whereas other people may have been raised in family, economic, or community conditions that make it very difficult for them to trust readily. If a person has experienced broken trust in the past, it will require a bigger leap of faith for him or her to trust in the future.

20   Ibid.

The second component of trust is the perception of competence, which comprises your confidence in both your ability and the abilities of others to perform as needed. For example, can someone keep a secret? Can someone be relied on to do a required task in the workplace properly and with the right level of service or quality?

The final component is the perception of intentions. Perception of intentions, as defined by Tway, is your perception that the actions, words, direction, or decisions of others are motivated by mutually serving rather than self-serving motives.[21] Have you ever worked with someone who intentionally slacked off to let others do more of the work? Have you ever had a manager or colleague who took credit for others' work? If you see this type of behavior in a person, you are less likely to trust his or her intentions in the future.

When considering how much to trust another person or an institution, such as a company, our ability to trust often depends on our conscious and unconscious assessment of these three components. First, any experiences you've had with the other person or business, plus your own life experiences, affect your capacity to trust. Second, you'll consider how competent you believe the person or institution is to actually carry through on whatever is required or whatever they have promised. And, finally, you'll think about whether you trust that the other person or institution has your best interests or their own best interests in mind. These three components play out in your life all the time, perhaps without your even noticing.

21   Ibid.

Our ability to share trust with our dogs follows this same model. First, given past experience with Panda, Garry is confident that he can leave Panda with full run of the house when Garry and his wife go out to dinner and that Panda will not chew up any furniture or make a mess. Garry also knows that Panda has a great capacity to trust family members because he allows them to pick him up and play with him. Second, Panda trusts that his family will give him food and shelter. Third, Panda trusts his family's intentions, and the family members trust his. When Panda approaches with a toy in his mouth, growling fiercely, Garry trusts Panda not to bite him. He knows Panda is not angry, but that he wants to play. When Garry or one of the kids wrestles the toy away, Panda knows that the person is not really going to keep it; rather, he is confident that he or she intends to toss it again for him to fetch.

We believe that most people would agree that at home and at work, trust is a vital element to good relationships and productivity. If we feel we can rely on others, cooperate with them to get things done, and communicate effectively, we are in a much better position to be happy and successful.

Whether you are at home or at work, the best way to maintain a trusting relationship is to ensure that you do not violate trust in the first place. However, if you have a low level of trust in someone, there are ways to try to improve the relationship. Apologizing when you are wrong is a positive first step. It is also helpful to be transparent in how you arrive at your decisions and to try to honestly

understand the perspective of the other person. You should also realize that if you have violated someone's trust, or vice versa, you will need to rebuild with many small actions over time.

COMPANIONSHIP

The final element of unconditional love identified by Laurie Puhn is companionship.[22] As previously noted, human beings and dogs are both social animals. Research has shown that both dogs and humans suffer if they are raised in isolation, without substantive contact and nurturing, which is vital for healthy development. Human infants are born absolutely helpless and unable to care for themselves. To survive, they depend on us for everything they need for many years. And, over the decades, we develop and learn about the world around us through our interactions with other people. Our connections to others are important not only to our survival but also to our happiness and success. We thrive on forming relationships with others.

The eminent psychologist Dr. Abraham Maslow even identified social relationships as a basic need of human beings.[23] And, frankly, all the other components of love—appreciation, respect, compassion, and trust—only make sense when considered in relation to someone else. It is wonderful to come home and have the love and support of our family companions: our spouses, our children, and, of course, our dogs. We are so lucky to have a place where we go to work and enjoy the companionship of our colleagues. Sharon shares that although her family's beloved Schnauzer passed away several years ago, the love and friendship of their friends and family keep them grounded in how important it is to know and feel the respect, appreciation, and companionship of those around us.

There are many things you can do to be a better companion to those you love. The secret is to enact the other four qualities of a loving relationship. Show genuine appreciation for others every time there is an opportunity. Demonstrate true respect for the thoughts, ideas, perspectives, values, and beliefs of others. Show compassion and empathy for the challenges others face. And don't forget to build a relationship on trust. Be open, honest, and tell the truth. Keep your commitments and remain faithful to those you love.

---

22 Neumann. (2011). Is Unconditional Love Unhealthy?
23 Cited in Baldwin, T, Bommer, W., & Rubin, R. (2008). *Developing Management Skills: What Great Managers Know and Do.* New York: McGraw-Hill, p. 131.

We all want to feel loved. We think about it, hope for it, fantasize about it, go to great lengths to achieve it, and feel that our lives are incomplete without it. One of the most difficult realities of living with dogs we love is that, as a rule, humans outlive our canine friends. For many dog owners, losing their furry friend is as traumatic as losing a family member. One of the best stories we recall about this issue was submitted in an online article titled, "Why Do Dogs Leave Earth First?"[24] The author, a veterinarian, describes being called to a family home to euthanize a ten-year-old Irish Wolfhound named Belker, who was dying of cancer. When the veterinarian arrived, the family had decided to allow their six-year-old son to observe the procedure because they thought he might learn something from the experience.

After Belker slipped peacefully away, the family and vet began discussing the unfortunate fact that animals' lives are so much shorter than humans' lives. The little boy, Shane, said quietly, "I know why." Startled, the family turned to Shane and asked him to explain. He said, "People are born so that they can learn to live a good life, like loving everybody all the time and being nice, right?" He then continued, "Well, dogs already know how to do that, so they don't have to stay as long."[25]

24   Retrieved December 12, 2012, from http://dogsnpawz.com/why-do-dogs-leave-earth-first/#.VVSoEZO-BZQ
25   *Ibid.*

Maybe that is the real reason dogs have been our best friend for so many thousands of years. Perhaps the most obvious reason that the dog has become man's best friend is that we know that when it comes to demonstrating love, a dog can always outperform us. Perhaps the lesson we can learn from dogs is to make sure that we love others as completely as possible. Do you need to tell someone you love them? Tell them now. Do you need to recognize someone's efforts at work for a job well done? Do it now. Do you have an opportunity to build trust with another person? Act now. Don't wait for the perfect time to show respect or be a true companion. Take heed from the short, intense lives of our dogs and show how much you can love now.

Thinking about Unconditional Love

Take a few minutes to think about what you have just read. Relate it to your life and the friends, family, coworkers, vendors, or others who cross your path on a daily basis. Jot down how you think you can apply what you have learned from your dog and others about love in your life.

Many people think love is simply an emotion, but, in fact, emotions are something we get from others. When we stop getting the response we desire, we often change our behavior. If you have to do something to receive love, then it is conditional. Dogs demonstrate their unconditional love by being our friend, paying attention, and spending valuable time with us. Think about how well you demonstrate your love to those who are important to you.

Who is someone to whom you need to actively demonstrate your love?

_____

Why does this person need to understand how much you love him or her?

_____

What will you do to appropriately demonstrate your love to this person?

_____

Love means being honest. If you truly love someone and want to foster its growth, you at times may need to say something uncomfortable. For example, you may need to avoid shielding someone from information or an experience that will help the person grow. In the space below, think of someone you love who you have sheltered or with whom you've avoided a conversation whose life would be greatly enhanced through what could be a difficult growth experience. What can you do or say (or not do or say) that will help him or her grow as a person?

Allow yourself to be loved. Many people find it easy to give love but not to receive love. Someone may feel as if he or she doesn't deserve to be loved, or that love should only be given to others. Wrong. The more often you honestly acknowledge and accept the love of others, the more you will be able to love. In the space below, list a few instances in which love was offered to you, but you minimized the action or avoided it altogether. How can you ensure you do not make this mistake again?

Love is limitless. Dogs know that they can give you all the love they have and still have plenty of love for everyone else. In our competitive society, we are conditioned to view love as a "limited pie"—in other words, if I give you love, then there is less for me to give to others. This is not true. Like our furry friends, we can get and give as much love as we want, and there will always be more give and receive. In the space below, note where you may have limited the amount of love you have given to someone and how you can change your mind-set to be more accepting in the future.

CHAPTER 5
FORGIVENESS

To err is human.
To forgive is canine...

My dogs forgive anger in me,
the arrogance in me, the brute
in me. They forgive everything
I do before I forgive myself.

—Guy de la Valdene

*G*arry recalls: "I stood in the field, glaring at Panda. He was happily running in great circles around me with an orange ball in his mouth. It was well below freezing, I was tired from a long day at the university, frustrated with the rush-hour drive home, and irritated that I had to take the dog for a walk when it was snowing. My most fervent wish was to be back at home, next to the fireplace, and yet here I was, stuck in the middle of an icy, cold field, being teased by a dog. Yet Panda was in no mood to leave. Over and over, he would stop 6 feet away, spit the ball out, hunker down in his play stance and 'woof' at me to 'just try and take it!'

"Every time I tried to grab the ball or catch Panda, he would snatch it up with his teeth and dance around gleefully, just out of reach. He plainly loved the fact that I could not get the ball, and he interpreted my increasingly frantic dashes to catch him and 'come here' snarls as clear evidence that this was the best game ever.

"After a dozen attempts at trying to grab him, and with my irritation growing, I finally tricked him into coming close enough that I could seize him by the collar and snap the leash on. Wet, frozen, and worn out, I growled, 'Bad dog! You are a bad, bad dog!' Panda cowered in response, looking bewildered. Seeing his reaction and feeling embarrassed, I began dragging him back toward the sidewalk and stalking home through the snow, with Panda hanging his head and glancing up at me every few steps as if to ask, 'What did I do wrong? Why are you so mad at me when we were having such a great time together?'

"As we walked, I began to reflect on the incident and my behavior, which, frankly, did not make me feel good. I knew I had overreacted and that Panda was simply doing what we did almost every time we came to the field during a walk: he was playing 'keep away' with me. Panda had been having a great time, but because of my long, tiring day, he was taking the brunt of my frustration. I had been unfair, and, by the time we got back to our house, I was feeling pretty ashamed.

"As we entered the house, I unsnapped the leash, and Panda scurried off to the living room while I went upstairs to shower and change. Afterward, I sat on the bed, still brooding about my behavior and contemplating how to make amends with Panda. I could picture him in my mind, moping around and ruminating on how unjustly I had behaved out in the field. But, to my surprise, he came bounding

up the stairs and launched himself onto the bed with a rubber bone in his mouth. Panda dropped the toy into my lap, raised his butt up into the air in his 'play with me' stance, put a big doggie grin on his face, and 'woofed' at me to try and take his toy. Here I was, agonizing over something that had happened thirty minutes earlier, and Panda had already forgiven me and moved on."

FORGIVENESS AND DOGS

As Garry's story illustrates, forgiving ourselves and others can be difficult. Occasionally, we also find it hard to let others forgive our own transgressions. Panda is representative of most dogs, who don't seem to have a problem forgiving or being forgiven. There appears to be a good reason for this fact. In her insightful book, *Inside of a Dog*, Dr. Alexandra Horowitz notes that the organization of a dog's brain and a human's brain is different.[1] According to Dr. Horowitz, the cerebral cortex in a dog's brain is not as fully developed at that of a human brain; this area of the brain supports higher order conceptual thinking. This difference makes dogs incapable of feeling guilt, which allows them to easily forgive transgressions. It is not that dogs don't remember wrongdoings; they just don't hold a grudge the way we humans do. Consequently, what we could perceive as a weakness in our dog turns out to contribute to one of the qualities we admire most in them: the ability to forgive.

1   Horowitz, A. (2010). *Inside of a Dog: What dogs See, Smell, and Know*. New York: Scribner.

If there ever were an animal that should hold grudges against humans, it certainly could be the dog. While most humans give dogs the care and nurturing they deserve, others are excessively abusive. Still others abandon their dogs at the local animal shelter when they are not wanted as if they were dropping off used clothes at the homeless shelter.

The lack of consideration and care provided to man's best friend in most puppy mills is appalling. In a *USA Today* article, Sharon Peters described her experience visiting the National Mill Dog Rescue in Peyton, Colorado.[2] This nonprofit organization rescues, rehabilitates, and finds homes for discarded breeding dogs and provides educational services to the general public about the cruel realities of the commercial dog-breeding industry. Peters described how she encountered more than 100 dogs who had been rescued from puppy mills, where they had been caged for years to produce litter after litter with very little food or water and no exercise. These neglected dogs received no veterinary care and little, if any, engagement with human beings.

As a result of this inhumane treatment, most dogs rescued by National Mill Dog Rescue are in dreadful states of health. After being housed in tiny enclosures for years, the dogs often have atrophied muscles due to lack of exercise, blindness from untreated eye infections, open sores on their skin, and teeth so rotten that, in many

2   Retrieved from http://usatoday30.usatoday.com/LIFE/usaedition/2011-10-11-Puppy-mill-psyche-YL-----_ST_U.htm

cases, infections have disintegrated their jawbones. Nonetheless, Peters explained that, when rescued, the dogs want love and affection, but they don't know how to go about getting it because no one has ever been nice to them.

Despite their horrendous, abusive treatment, dogs who have known nothing but neglect, pain, and suffering from humans learn to forgive us. The founder of National Mill Dog Rescue, Theresa Strader, comments on this amazing ability of dogs to forgive, stating, "Once they're no longer in pain or starving [and] once they get regular doses of care and love, they come around."[3] How can it be that dogs who have suffered such abuse from human beings can learn to forgive and trust again? How do they learn to trust that the hand that reaches out to care for them is doing so in love, not to injure or harm?

Garry's experience with Panda at the beginning of this chapter led us to consider the difference in how dogs and humans respond when given the opportunity to forgive. Dr. Horowitz's research indicates that dogs don't engage in the same level of complex thought as we do, nor do they contemplate what has happened to them in the past.[4] While Garry was in the shower, pondering what a jerk he had been, Panda had already gotten over the incident.

3   Ibid.
4   Horowitz, A. (2010). Inside of a Dog.

Personal Activity:

FORGIVENESS

Can you think of a time when you believe your dog forgave you for something you did, such as accidentally stepping on his or her paw or tail?

_____

What did you do to show your remorse?

_____

What did the dog do that indicated you were forgiven?

WHAT IS FORGIVENESS?

We have all been hurt or angered by what someone else has done or said, whether it was intentional or not. True forgiveness is a decision to let go of our anger and our desire to punish the other person or teach him or her a lesson. The act of forgiving does not mean that we forget the offense or hurt, but rather that we choose not to dwell on it and instead focus on more positive aspects of our life. Forgiveness is what allows us to move forward. We want to stress that forgiveness does not mean that we deny the other person's responsibility for having hurt us, and it certainly does not seek to diminish or excuse the wrong done. We can forgive a person for something he or she did without excusing or forgetting that the person did it.

It is easier to talk about forgiving others than it is to actually do it. When we are hurt by someone we love or trust, it is natural to become angry, hurt, and confused.

Sometimes this can be a real or perceived slight that goes back years. Not too long ago, an associate of ours mentioned that her twentieth high school class reunion was being held in a few weeks. When we asked if she planned to go, she replied, "No. When I was in high school, there was this girl who started dating a boy I was dating at the time. It really made me mad, and I don't want to run into her."

Wow. It's twenty years later, and this woman is married to a wonderful husband and has a delightful family, but she is still harboring a grudge so enormous that she is willing to pass up the chance to see dozens of other former classmates. How many other real or imagined affronts has this woman been carrying around on her shoulders? As this example suggests, if you dwell on hurtful events, negative feelings crowd out the positive feelings and opportunities. In this case, this woman has spent years wallowing in her own sense of bitterness and injustice over something that admittedly may have been a big deal at the time but, in the grand scheme of life, was pretty darn minor. She could decide to laugh at how silly she and the other girl both had been at the time.

Dogs are very good at forgiving us when accidents and misunderstandings occur. As the foregoing example suggests, we humans are often inclined to brood over real or imagined offenses for years and even decades. (In some countries, various ethnic groups have harbored grudges against each other for hundreds and even thousands

of years). Imagine how confusing this must be to dogs. Suppose, for example, you come home to find that your dog chewed up one of your shoes or got into the trash. Once you remove the shoe from his mouth or clean the mess from the trash can, the dog will have filed the incident away and moved on. Consider how puzzling it must be to the dog to find that hours or even days later, you continue to glare at him and growl "bad dog" periodically. What an amazing waste of time and energy this scenario is for both you and the dog.

Pup the Schnauzer was usually eager to forgive and forget any of Sharon's transgressions, such as leaving him when she went to work or go shopping. That being said, Pup often exhibited his "human" characteristics when Sharon would leave him home for longer periods of time. She would drive up and see him sitting in his favorite chair in front of the window, watching for her. Sharon never found out for sure if he stayed there while she was gone or if he heard the car coming and hurriedly got into the chair to watch her come in.

Here is the interesting part of life with Pup: When Sharon came in, he would jump down, run to her, smile, dance around a couple of times, and wait for his kiss. Then, as if something had stuck him, he would stop cold, glare at Sharon, stomp his foot, stiffen his neck, and storm off, leaving her watching as he smoked off

down the hall."Sharon always enjoyed Pup's little forays into being "human" and holding a grudge because within fifteen minutes or so he would come back, acting as if nothing had happened, and revert to his loving, adorable little self.

We often reflect upon how many times our dogs forgive us for leaving them for hours, days, or even weeks with no explanation at all. We have no idea what is going through our dogs' minds when we leave them to go to work for the day or when we drop them off at the kennel for a week when the family goes on vacation. Our dogs have no idea why we left or when we will return, but when we do, they are absolutely thrilled to see us, and they quickly forgive us for having left in the first place. Perhaps it is time to take a moment to learn something about forgiveness from our best friend.

Too many of us go through life with grudges for wrongs that have been done to us long ago. This results in high levels of stress, which leads to negativity, which may spill over into other relationships. For some people, harboring petty grudges and blaming others becomes a way of being, and they live an existence in which they feel persecuted and wronged. The worst thing about an unforgiving person is that he or she is often the one most damaged by the intolerance toward the person against whom he or she holds a grudge. And how often have you learned that the person against whom you have a grudge does not even realize he or she did anything to hurt your feelings? It is also possible that the person is well aware of what he or she did but does not care. You are the one holding on to the resentment that is harming you and you alone.

WHY FORGIVE?

Forgiving others is a basic principle for a healthy, positive life. When we are tolerant of peoples' shortcomings and give them the benefit of the doubt, we open ourselves to greater understanding instead of making judgments that may not be accurate. We never know precisely why other people do what they do. What we think we see clearly is often not what is going on at all. Perhaps the person is under a great deal of stress and is having a hard time dealing with it. Or perhaps the person intended for his or her words or actions to be in your best interest. Garry recounts an incident that occurred in his previous role in the training department of a high-technology firm. One day, he was attending a staff meeting that included members of the manufacturing team. During the meeting, Garry

shared information relating to the success of a training event that had been conducted for manufacturing managers and technicians. Brian, a senior technician and generally a strong supporter of the training department, began making very disparaging remarks about the nature of the training, its effectiveness, and Garry's competence in coordinating and teaching the workshops. Garry felt this was a brazen and unwarranted personal attack, as well as being very much against the standards of conduct that employees followed in meetings. Garry swallowed his inclination to lash out at Brian and instead asked Brian to explain his thoughts in greater detail. Brian brusquely declined, saying, "There is no point in me saying anything. Nothing we suggest makes any difference anyway."

Garry could see that everyone was wondering if he was going to "put Brian in his place." However, Brian's behavior was so out of character that Garry sensed there was something more to the incident; rather than press his questions or put Brian on the spot in front of everyone, he simply moved forward with the agenda. Brian remained sullen and uncommunicative throughout the rest of the meeting. Afterward, Garry asked Brian to stay behind and sat down with him.

"Brian," Garry began, "I could certainly see that you feel strongly that we need to improve the training being provided to you and your colleagues. Your opinion is important to me because you are on the front line and a good observer of what works and what doesn't. I also know that everyone really looks up to you on the manufacturing floor." Brian fidgeted and doodled on his notepad but did not look up or proffer a response. Garry decided to probe a little further and said, "It will not make me mad to hear that we can improve; I would really like to understand what we can do better. Would you mind sharing what you have observed?"

At this point, Brian put his pen down, clasped his hands in front of him, and looked up with misty eyes. "Garry," he said, "I apologize. There's nothing wrong with the training. Last night, my wife told me she wants a divorce, and I am so upset that I don't know what else to do. I am so sorry, but I took my frustration out on all of you during the meeting. I feel stupid and embarrassed for reacting so thoughtlessly. I hope you can forgive me for having criticized you so strongly in front of all our colleagues."

You probably feel the way Garry did at this point. Garry was no longer mad at Brian. Rather, Garry could empathize with him. Garry understood how he must feel and could reach out and offer emotional support at a time when Brian needed it. It was very easy for Garry to forgive Brian. In fact, that incident helped cement their friendship, and Brian continued to be a great supporter of the company's training efforts. Of course, the training staff went out of their way to ensure that Brian and his work teams received their full support.

As this incident suggests, being willing to forgive provides freedom from all sorts of destructive emotions that can create barriers between others and cause us personal stress, unhappiness, depression, and even illness. If we can put the same amount of energy into giving others the benefit of the doubt, we can create more engaging, trust-based relationships and be happier and healthier in our own lives.

WHY IS IT HARD TO FORGIVE?

Forgiveness expert Dr. Everett Worthington, Jr. of Virginia Commonwealth University believes that "when it comes to day-to-day forgiveness, dogs are our masters."[5] Whether at work or at home, forgiveness is often very hard to bestow on others or on ourselves. One of the reasons is that we may believe that the person who offended us does not deserve our forgiveness. We may also feel that the

---

5   McClure, M. (2012, February 11). Forgiveness: To Err is Human, to Forgive is Canine. *Garden Island.* Retrieved from http://thegardenisland.com/lifestyles/pets/furgiveness-to-err-is-human-to-forgive-canine/article_de0de614-554a-11e1-b0fb-0019bb2963f4.html

other person deserves to be punished for committing an injustice against us. And sometimes we are simply reluctant to let go of our anger. If you are angry, you can feel self-righteous and smug in the knowledge that someone else hurt you, and, by golly, he or she is not going to get away with it. Frankly, it can feel good to carry around that chip on your shoulder, can't it?

But psychologists and counselors stress that forgiving someone else for an injustice does not mean that you are letting that person get away with it. First, forgiveness is not the same as forgetting. Forgiveness is the process of acknowledging that someone did you wrong and then moving to a place where you can remember the injustice without feeling resentment or pursuing revenge. Second, forgiveness is not excusing an injustice to you or others, and it certainly does not mean that you have to put yourself in the position of being hurt again. You can forgive someone and still take healthy steps to ensure that you are protecting yourself from future harm. Finally, forgiveness does not necessarily mean that you reconcile with someone. Reconciliation means that two people work together to understand and acknowledge what occurred, recognize that the relationship is worth saving, and then agree, figuratively speaking, to "bury the hatchet."

HOW CAN YOU FORGIVE?

Because we have such a great capacity to remember when we are hurt and the propensity to hold it against another person, we are much different from dogs. As noted earlier, because dogs have a different brain structure than humans do, they forgive and forget much more easily. For example, Garry noticed that the kitchen needed to be swept. Panda always takes an interest in this chore because it is likely that the person with the broom will sweep out a little bit of kibble or some other food particles that have fallen into a corner or under the table. Consequently, as Garry moved along, Panda was darting here and there around Garry's feet to see what tasty morsel he could find. On this day, as Garry moved backward, he accidently stepped on Panda's paw. Yes, Panda should not have been there, but it clearly hurt him.

Panda yelped and limped to the living room with one paw held up while glancing back over his shoulder at Garry with big, mournful eyes. Garry stopped sweeping, went to Panda, and began petting him and saying the same type of soothing words you would offer to a child: "Oh, Panda! I am so sorry. I didn't mean to step on your paw. Let me look at it." Panda began to lick Garry's hand to let Garry know he was not angry. Ten minutes later, it was as if the incident never happened,

although Garry has noticed that Panda tries to keep more distance when he sweeps the floor.

Cats, however, can be totally unforgiving, as one of Sharon's friend's cats has let her know. Sharon's friend had asked Sharon to watch the cat, Annabelle, while the family went on vacation. One day, Sharon went to their home and started the usual rounds of cleaning the litter box and ensuring the cat had water and food. Unfortunately, Annabelle got between Sharon and her feet, and Sharon stepped on Annabelle's paw. Sharon recalls that the cat bawled as if her leg had been cut off. The cat went to her water bowl and, while glaring at Sharon, stuck her paw in the water and moved it up and down several times. Sharon went to Annabelle and began petting her head and back, telling her how sorry she was for stepping on her paw. Annabelle took her foot out of the water, limped off across the room to the laundry room, jumped up on top of the clothes on top of the washer, and turned her back to Sharon. The cat did not show any interest in Sharon until the next day, when Sharon came back to take care of her. Sharon reports that it still took Annabelle quite a few days to act as if Sharon were worthy of her attention and any affection. Maybe that illustrates one of the differences between dogs and cats.

FIVE CRITICAL TASKS FOR EARNING FORGIVENESS

While Panda and other dogs are able to forgive very quickly, it usually takes us a little longer to get over the feeling of hurt over a real or imagined injustice. When you feel that you have been wronged, there are five steps you should consider to determine how to react to the situation.

- First, take a step back and consider your assumptions and beliefs about the situation. If you feel wronged, does it seem as though the person was truly acting out of malice, or could it have been unintentional? If it is your assessment that the person did act out of malice, approach the person and explain how his or her actions made you feel and the repercussions of those actions. With any luck, the person will apologize and/or explain his or her intentions to help clarify any misunderstanding.

- Second, think about what pain, negative feelings, or discomfort you may have caused. Are you certain that you did not do or say something to instigate or contribute to the situation?

- Third, if it turns out you were at fault in some way, apologize genuinely, nondefensively, and responsibly.

- Fourth, begin to take action to earn trust back. You might ask, "What can I do to make this up to you?"

- Fifth, forgive yourself for injuring another person. This reminds me of a comment made by Lisa Hunt, a dynamic sales executive with Hilton Hotels and a sincere lover of dogs. Lisa observed, "One of the best lessons I learned about myself and my dog took place when I attended puppy training. One of the other people in the class asked the trainer what he should do if the dog ever has an accident in the house. Without missing a beat, the trainer said, 'If your puppy ever makes a mistake on the floor, you should roll up a newspaper tightly, go to the dog, and hit yourself on the side of the head several times for not paying attention to the puppy's behavior and needs. Then forgive yourself and the puppy and pay better attention next time.'[6] Isn't that great?

Albert Schweitzer, one of the greatest philosophers of our time, has this to say about forgiveness: "I am obliged to exercise unlimited forgiveness because, if I

---

6   Interview with Lisa Hunt, May, 2013.

did not forgive, I should be untrue to myself, in that I should thus act as if I were not guilty in the same ways the other has been guilty with regard to me. I must forgive the lies directed against myself, because my own life has been so many times blotted by lies; I must forgive the lovelessness, the hatred, the slander, the fraud, the arrogance which I encounter, since I myself have so often lacked love, hated, slandered, defrauded, and been arrogant. I must forgive without noise or fuss."[7]

The world dogs inhabit is one that is amazingly forgiving. Dogs are quick to forgive the wrongs foisted upon them and are quick to rebuild damaged relationships. Thinking back on the research by Dr. Horowitz, having a brain as complex as ours sometimes seems to be more of a burden than a blessing. Sometimes our unwillingness to forgive, to say "I'm sorry," or to accept an apology from others gets in our way of building and sustaining good relationships with others. The amazing capacity for forgiveness is still one of the greatest gifts that dogs have given us.

7   Cited in Straw, D. (2003) What Animals Teach Me About Forgiveness. *Soulful Living*. Retrieved from http://www.
soulfulliving.com/animals_teach_forgiveness.htm

Malachy McCourt said, "Resentment is like taking poison and waiting for the other person to die."[8] Is there a grudge or something that happened that you still agonize over and from which you would benefit if you were to forgive the other person? Identify that grudge here.

What are you gaining by not forgiving the other person?

What would you gain if you did forgive the other person?

Forgiveness can be offered to others, and it can also be applied to ourselves. Is there something you did in the past that you know was wrong and for which you have been beating yourself up? Sometimes it is better to acknowledge that you made an error, but also to recognize that you have learned from the error, forgiven yourself, and moved on. In the space below, describe what happened or what you did, how it impacted yourself and/or others, what you learned from this error, and the benefit of forgiving yourself and moving on.

8   Retrieved June 1, 2015, from www.forbes.com/sites/amyanderson/2015/04/07/resentment-is-like-taking-poison-and-waiting-for-the-other-person-to-die/

CHAPTER 6
POSITIVE ATTITUDE

When an 85-pound mammal licks your tears away [and] then tries to sit on your lap, it's hard to feel sad.

—KRISTAN HIGGINS

Happiness is a warm puppy.

—CHARLES M. SCHULZ

$\mathcal{A}$ long time ago, there was a small village with a wonderful attraction that people came from miles around to see: the house of 1,000 mirrors. One day, two dogs approached the village on two different paths. The first to enter the town was a happy dog. When the little dog learned of the house of mirrors, he could not wait to see it. As soon as he arrived at the house, he bounded up to the front door and looked expectantly inside. To his amazement, he found himself staring at 1,000 other cheerful dogs, all wagging their tails just as fast as he was wagging his. He smiled back and was delighted to see he was answered with just as many warm, friendly smiles. "How wonderful," the dog said to himself. "Every dog in this village is so positive and welcoming! Any community with so many happy dogs is going to be a great place for me, too," he said as he trotted into the village.

Several minutes later, the second dog, who believed that the world was cruel and hateful, came upon the house of 1,000 mirrors. He slowly climbed the steps to the front door with his head held low, ever ready for danger or attack, and looked inside. When he saw 1,000 unfriendly dogs baring their teeth at him with suspicious eyes, he spun quickly around and ran, with his tail between his legs, back

to the edge of town. "It's lucky that I got away from such a horrible house!" he said to himself. "Any village with so many unfriendly dogs would be a terrible place to live." And with that, he slunk down the road all alone.[1]

Sir Ken Robinson, internationally recognized leader in the development of creativity, innovation, and human resources and author of *The Element: Finding Your Passion Changes Everything* and *Out of Our Minds: Learning to Be Creative*, tells a wonderful story about a young girl who rarely paid attention in her first-grade class. One day, the class was tasked with a drawing project. All the children were busily working on their individual efforts when the teacher noticed the little girl at the back of the room, totally engaged in her drawing. The teacher walked to the back of the room and asked, "Annie, what are you working on?"

Annie kept drawing as she replied, "A picture of God."

Taken aback, the teacher said, "But, Annie, no one knows what God looks like."

Without looking up, Annie responded, "They will in a minute."[2]

We find these two stories compelling because both convey a delightful message that we believe is true in our lives: your attitude has a lot to do with how you view the world and how others view you. Have you ever noticed how being around positive people makes you feel better, too? Isn't there a noticeable difference between people with a great attitude and those who perpetually believe the sky is falling? Positive people light up a room with their energy and encourage those with whom they interact to feel upbeat and happier for having been around them. This is because when we give positive energy to others, it seems to come back to us two-, three-, or even tenfold.

1   Retrieved from www.great-inspirational-quotes.com/the-house-of-1000-mirrors.html
2   Retrieved June 7, 2015, from www.ted.com/talks/ken_robinson_says_schools_kill_creativity

We believe that the way others respond to us is often a reflection of how we treat them. Our face and the faces of others in the world are like the mirrors in the house visited by the two dogs. If we are distrusting, disrespectful, depressed, and ill tempered, we tend to surround ourselves with like-minded people. If we expect the world to be unfair, unpleasant, and disagreeable, we see evidence to support our belief all around us. That is hardly a positive and uplifting way to go through life.

With few exceptions, dogs appear to view the world with love, motivation, and anticipation. For example, Garry relates that when he gets up in the morning and in the evening when he returns home, Panda is thrilled to see him. Garry's wife says that when Panda hears the garage door opening, the dog begins to bark excitedly and dance around the door to the garage. When Garry opens the door, Panda runs in circles around Garry, wiggling with joy. Panda's positive attitude toward his family and the day ahead is unmistakable in his behavior.

The questions you should ask yourself are: What kind of reflection do you see in the faces of people you meet? Do your face and your behavior project an attitude of hope, joy, and optimism or one of doubt, depression, and distrust? In this chapter, we are going to explore what we admire about our dogs' attitudes and how you can enhance the power of your own attitude.

As we researched this book, we ran across the following quote from an unknown author: "A behavior is only short lived in the scheme of things, but an attitude can be yours for life." This sage advice that our attitudes have lasting value was confirmed by an experience Garry had as a young lieutenant in the United States Air Force. At the time, Garry was stationed at Mather Air Force Base in Sacramento, California, serving in the Navigator Instructor Training School. This was a wonderful job, and Garry had

the great pleasure of working with many very talented personnel from the Marines, Army, Navy, Coast Guard, and National Oceanic and Atmospheric Administration as well as with military personnel from more than thirty nations.

Garry thoroughly enjoyed his time in the military and bought his first home in Rancho Cordova, a suburb of Sacramento. This first real estate purchase was a 12-by-60-foot used mobile home with a tiny little lawn and a great flower garden at the front of the trailer. To Garry, it was a palace and a wonderful change from apartment life.

Garry soon learned that he knew little about gardening and was delighted when an elderly woman across the street from him took a humorous and lively interest in helping him keep the flowers alive. Grandma Radke, as she insisted on being called, spent hours coaching him about when he should water and fertilize, which plants to pull up, and which plants to leave alone. She also dispensed valuable wisdom when appropriate. In return for her advice, Garry mowed her lawn, worked on her flowerbed, helped her with odd jobs here and there, and paid attention when she had some morsel of insight to impart.

One day, Garry was pulling weeds in the garden as Grandma Radke looked on. He stopped and looked up at her and said, "Grandma Radke, today is my twenty-fifth birthday. It occurs to me that I have now been alive for a quarter of a century. You have lived more than three times as long. I wonder if you have any advice for a young guy like me."

She thought for a minute and then said, "Garry, in all seriousness, the most important thing I've learned in life is that your attitude is everything. I've lived eighty-seven years so far, and I hope to live another ten or twenty. I've seen it all: babies born, children growing up, graduations, sicknesses, wonderful accomplishments, and great failures. I have seen divorce, illness, and calamity. And, of course, I have seen death take friends and family too often."

She paused and gazed at him before continuing. "But, Garry, I have also learned that life is very fair to each of us. I've seen some people become rich and successful only to let it go to their heads and destroy their lives with alcohol, drugs, or some craziness that leads to divorce and the loss of their family. On the other hand, I've seen some people experience great misfortune and become stronger for it. It's your attitude that helps you or keeps you from moving successfully through those times."

Today, with six decades of experience behind him, Garry can attest that the advice Grandma Radke shared then is still some of the best advice he ever received. Even now, almost forty years later, Garry still reflects on the wisdom behind those

clear eyes that looked at him long ago through eight decades of life. Grandma Radke was right; good and bad things happen to all of us, and it is not what happens to us that makes the difference in our lives. What makes the difference is our attitude toward what happens. Her advice is echoed by Dr. Stephen Covey, who observed that we are all responsible for our own attitudes and decisions. Dr. Covey points out that the word "responsible" comes from the combination of "response" and "able."[3] In other words, we are each able to choose our own response, and this is certainly true for our attitudes. As with the other six secrets of happiness demonstrated by dogs, attitude is another trait we admire greatly in our canine companions.

EVERYTHING IS AN ADVENTURE

One of Garry's colleagues at the university, Dr. Gary Stroud, is a gifted professor who has held a number of impressive positions in various businesses and within the community. Dr. Stroud is one of those rare individuals who comes with a wonderful mix of practical life and business experience along with homespun wisdom. He and his wife, Gwen, have a wonderful dog named Kate Jackson. Kate Jackson is a friendly mixed-breed dog who will be your friend for life if you rub her

3   Covey, S. *The Seven Habits of Highly Effective People*. (1989). New York, NY: Simon and Schuster, p. 71.

belly. Dr. Stroud remarked about his furry family member: "You know what I like most about Kate Jackson? She reminds me of that old saying 'if you are a hammer, then everything looks like a nail.' Well, if you are Kate Jackson, everything looks like an adventure!" Doesn't that sum up a dog's attitude about life? Everything is an adventure. Kate Jackson, Panda, and every other dog we have met certainly embody this adage.

Garry notes that he is consistently surprised at how excited Panda can become at the prospect of…well, anything! When Garry or his wife go to the store for thirty minutes and then return, Panda responds with the enthusiasm of a dozen six-year olds waking up on Christmas morning or the first day of Hanukkah. He can't wait to see what is in each grocery bag. He jumps around, focusing intently on each bag as they unpack, and he "woofs" softly as though he believes that Garry or Lauren will whip out a huge T-bone steak just for him at any moment.

Anytime Panda and Garry go outside, it is an extraordinary adventure. It is going to be fun. It is going to be the best day of Panda's life. And it soon becomes totally clear that Panda views any walk outside very differently from how Garry does. Garry relates that when he wants to take Panda for a walk, Garry tends to think of the walk in linear, goal-oriented human terms. In Garry's mind, he and Panda will walk out of the house, go down the block, turn left, stride along for another 200 yards, and arrive at the park where (again, in Garry's mind) Panda will quickly do his business. Garry will then be a good neighbor, pick up after Panda, be patient for a few minutes while Panda smells where a half-dozen other dogs have peed, and then they will walk home.

That's how it goes in Garry's head. Not so for Panda. While Garry envisions a specific route that goes from point A to point B and back, Panda actually follows a path that, from Garry's point of view, is very chaotic and meandering. From the moment they step outside, Panda is zigzagging one way and then another. First, he is totally enthralled by smelling something on one side of the sidewalk, and then there is something equally thrilling on the other side. Next, he sees a blowing leaf that is just the most amazing sight ever, and he has to chase it down. Then, up ahead, is that a stick? He has to check that out, too, and—marvel of marvels—he sees another stick! And just when Garry thinks they are making some progress, Panda has to circle back to some enchanting spot 10 feet back just to get another whiff of an amazing smell permeating the ground or the base of a tree.

And, as if all of this were not exciting enough, sometimes Garry and Panda have the fantastic luck to meet another mom or dad walking his or her dog, and the excitement intensifies by a factor of twenty. Panda and the other dog are both

reduced to wiggling, slobbering, rear-smelling ecstasy. When the two dogs have gained the maximum level of joy from sniffing each other's nether regions, each simply must express his delight by tinkling on some particularly magical spot in the dirt so that the other dog can smell and then tinkle on the same spot. Of course, there is a great deal of tail wagging, posturing, and/or leaping about in play to celebrate the tinkle ceremony.

When we go to somewhere different—a new park, for example—well, in dog terms, this must be what heaven is like. Everything is new. New leaves to smell, new sticks to chase and chew up, perhaps new dogs to meet, and maybe even the scents of other creatures that don't live close to us (turkeys, opossums, raccoons, deer, and the like).

You get the picture. Panda expects the world to be fun and worth exploring. He expects new encounters to be wonderful. Something as simple as a walk around the block, a trip to the store, or a visit to the local park is a wondrous and momentous event. Show Panda a stick, an old leaf, or a smelly spot on the ground, and he is thrilled. Panda's attitude is absolutely in the right place.

Personal Activity 1:

POSITIVE ATTITUDE

We realize that dogs have much simpler minds and fewer demands on their time than we do. That said, why is the apparent positive attitude dogs that consistently display a quality you admire?

Notes:

Yes, I am making light of Panda's approach to taking a walk, meeting another dog, or greeting us when we come home, but, frankly, my life is better for it. I am not embarrassed to acknowledge that if our walks went like I planned, they would be quite dull. Thanks to Panda, my awareness of the world around me is widened when I am with him. I can't help but watch what he discovers with his profoundly better sense of smell, and he often finds things that I would have missed entirely. Also, because Panda is so willing to engage with others, I am able to meet adults and children throughout our neighborhood.

THE POWER OF A POSITIVE ATTITUDE

On the surface, attitude is how you communicate your mood to others. With a positive attitude, you see the better side of life, become optimistic, and expect the best to happen. Sir Ken Robinson explains this in the following way:

"Attitude is our personal perspective on ourselves and our circumstances—our angle on things, our disposition and emotional point of view. Many things affect our attitudes, including our basic character, our spirit, our sense of self-worth, the perceptions of those around us, and their expectations of us. An interesting indicator of our basic attitude is how we think of the role of luck in our life.

"People who love what they do often describe themselves as lucky. People who think they're not successful in their lives often say they've been unlucky. Accidents and randomness play some part in everybody's lives. But there's more to luck than pure chance. High achievers often share similar attitudes such as perseverance, self-belief, optimism, ambition, and frustration. How we perceive our circumstances and how we create and take opportunities depends largely on what we expect of ourselves.[4]"

When you are optimistic, you transmit positive energy, and people respond favorably. Of course, no one can be positive all the time. As Sir Robinson suggests,

---

4   Robinson, Sir Ken. (2014). Finding Your Passion. *Fireside* 44 (3 July – September), p. 23.

bad things do happen to good people. A positive attitude is not an act; it must be genuine. And, frankly, at times it is impossible to be positive in the face of some setbacks. Although Panda is in a positive state 99 percent of the time, he is not overjoyed when a family member vacuums, when he needs a bath, or when it's time to have his toenails clipped. But their previous dog, Spot, thought the vacuum cleaner was the best toy ever! Spot also loved getting a bath and could care less if you cut his nails because he simply interpreted these tasks as additional opportunities for him to get attention. Just like with people, what appeals to one dog does not necessarily appeal to another.

PERSONAL BENEFITS

As you might guess, a positive attitude helps us cope more easily with our daily affairs. Decades of research indicates that people with positive attitudes do better in all aspects of life, including school, sports, business, relationships, and politics. The reasons are simple: a positive attitude is proactive and affirming. Who would vote for a politician who spouts nothing but gloom and doom? What coach gets in front of his or her players and says, "There is no use in trying. We're going to get crushed!"? And salespeople know that they must expect to get a certain number of refusals for every sale that they finally close.

Research also suggests that a positive attitude can contribute to greater lifelong health. In one study conducted by the *Journal of Personality and Social Psychology*, researchers surveyed ninety-nine men at age twenty-five and rated their degree of optimism about life. Researchers surveyed the same men again at the age of sixty-five and found that the optimists in the group had survived for the previous forty years in much better health than those who reported more negative attitudes toward life.[5]

A related study conducted by the Harvard School of Public Health links a positive attitude to lower risk of heart disease in men and women. Further, Dr. Peter Norvid at the Amita Health Adventist Medical Center in Hinsdale, Illinois, notes, "Optimistic people live longer, have closer personal relationships, and are able to deal with the negative things that happen to them in a way that allows them to continue to be able to be there for others so that others can help them."[6]

Research also suggests that the news for people with negative attitudes is not good. Studies conducted at the Mayo Clinic indicate that even after adjusting for age and gender, people with a negative attitude suffered a higher risk factor for early death. The reason for the difference is explained by Ken Budd, former executive editor of *AARP The Magazine*. "It's believing in good times during bad times," says Budd. "It's feeling grateful for what you have instead of lamenting what you lack. It's believing not simply that the positive outweighs the negative in life, but that we can create positive feelings and actions; that we have the power to make ourselves happy and content."[7]

The message we should glean from all of this research is that a positive attitude does make a difference in your life. And a key aspect of this is that what you focus on is important; the difference between what we can perceive and what we actually perceive differs. Best-selling author and motivational speaker Anthony Robbins demonstrates this principle with a simple activity when he asks those attending his seminar to look around and count the number of items of green clothing they can see on the people around them. After a minute, he then asks them how many items of red clothing they saw. As you might guess, most people can't even begin to answer the question because they were looking for green, not red, clothing.

5   Vogin, G. D. (n.d.) Living on the Sunny Side: Be Happy. WebMD Retrieved July 30, 2015, from www.webmd.com/balance/features/living-on-sunny-side

6   Norvid, P. (2013). A Positive Mental Attitude Benefits Health, Longevity and Quality of Life. *Chicago Tribune*. Retrieved from www.chicagotribune.com/classified/realestate/chi-primetime-pma-022611-story.html

7   Retrieved from www.chicagotribune.com/classified/realestate/chi-primetime-pma-022611-story.html

His point is that you see what you are looking for. If you go through life looking for what is wrong with life, then that is what you will see. If you look for what is wonderful, fulfilling, and positive, you will see that instead.[8]

Garry's father was a colonel in the United States Air Force and, as a "military brat," Garry learned from personal experience that a positive attitude makes a huge difference in child-rearing. Like most military families, Garry's moved quite often—generally every two to three years. Without fail, when the family received notice of a pending move to a new location somewhere in the United States or overseas, Garry, his brother, and his sister would wail, "We don't want to go! This is the best place we've ever lived!" Their parents would empathize, confirm that the current duty station was wonderful, and then begin discussing how great the new location would be. They actively engaged the three children in conducting research at the library to learn about attractions and things to do at the new location. Garry's mother and father maintained an upbeat attitude both before the move and when they arrived at the new military base.

Regardless of his parents' efforts, Garry reports that he and his siblings always hated the new location for the first six months and were quite vocal in their displeasure. But two years later, when the family would receive orders to move

8   Robbins, A. (2006). Retrieved June 8, 2015, from www.ted.com/talks/tony_robbins_asks_why_we_do_what_we_do

again, the current location was the best place the children had ever lived, and they did not want to leave. Guess what? Once again, Garry's mother and father would become the epitome of positive motivation for the new move.

Second, Garry's parents never criticized or belittled the children's career aspirations as they grew up. Instead, his parents listened to each child's career dreams and helped them explore the possibilities. For example, if Garry approached his mother and said, "Mom, I want to be a firefighter when I grow up," she would say, "Great! Let's go to the fire station and talk to some firefighters." And then she would arrange a visit. Garry would meet the firefighters, tour the fire station, sit in the cab of a fire truck, slide down the pole, pet the fire dog, and return home convinced that would be his life's ambition. Six months later, Garry would approach her and solemnly declare, "Mom, I have decided I want to be a doctor." She would clap her hands together and say, "Wonderful! I know a woman who is a great physician. I will arrange for you to talk with her to learn what it takes to be a doctor." And so it would go. Regardless of what the three siblings declared was their current career goal (Indian chief, ballerina, chef, architect, rock star, teacher, cowboy, rocket scientist, fisherman, etc.), mom would find a way for them to talk to someone in that field or conduct research to learn about that profession. Her message was never stated openly, but it was clear in her attitude: it is OK to dream and explore.

The positive attitude demonstrated by Garry's parents extends to others as well. Like many young adults, Sir Richard Branson struggled in school and dropped out at age sixteen. This did not keep him from achieving great entrepreneurial success in the music

industry and other sectors, which have made him a billionaire. His Virgin Group holds more than 200 companies, including the recent Virgin Galactic, a space tourism company. Branson is also known for his adventurous spirit and sporting achievements, such as crossing oceans in a hot-air balloon. He gives his mother credit for his success. "My mum has always had a keen entrepreneurial streak and still does today. When I was a child, she inspired me to take risks in all manner of business ventures. Most of them did not work out (notably growing Christmas trees and breeding budgerigars), but the lessons learned were invaluable." Branson goes on to say, "The amount of time people spend looking back on failed projects has always astounded me. If we were to add up all the hours spent regretting mistakes and use that time to develop new ideas, who knows how many brilliant new businesses would be created?"[9]

ATTITUDE AND WORK

Mark Poeppelman is the executive director for the Columbus International Program, a nonprofit organization that links businesses and professionals from across the globe to share ideas and best practices and create positive relationships. As you might guess, a job like Poeppelman's requires someone who is supremely positive and able to adapt to the nuances of a wide variety of people and cultures. When Garry needs advice, he has found that Poeppelman is one of those people who will give you his attention and help find a positive way to solve any problem. One snowy afternoon, when the two men were having lunch, Garry shared how he was progressing on this chapter and asked Poeppelman if he thought that dogs had positive attitudes as well and, if so, whether it influenced his outlook at work.

"Of course," Poeppelman quickly replied, "I really appreciate my dog's attitude. My wife and I have a three-year-old Soft Coated Wheaten Terrier named Opie

9   Branson, R. (2013, February 26). Best Advice: No Regrets, and Practicing What You Preach. Retrieved from http://whootafrica.com/best-advice-no-regrets-and-practicing-what-you-preach-by-richard-branson/

and our mood at home is lightened every day and our burdens seem less important when he is in the room. Opie reminds my wife and me all the time that how we look at life has a lot to do with how much we enjoy it. Opie has a great attitude, and it rubs off on us." Mark went on to say, "I have a great job that provides me the opportunity to work with amazing people from all over the world. Our mission at the International Program is to build bridges between cultures. Having a positive attitude like Opie's is a must for this business."[10]

As Mark says so eloquently, nowhere is a positive attitude appreciated more than at work. Mark is an effective leader in his own right and also very effective in developing leadership in others. Being a leader is a subtle thing. Because of the way organizations are structured, many people associate leadership with being "in charge." They equate the "leader" with being someone who has formal authority over others.

Leadership is much more than an appointed position. When we teach about leadership in our undergraduate or graduate programs, we define it as a role that all people in an organization possess. We believe that everyone is a leader—

10   Interview with Mark Poeppelman, April 16, 2013.

certainly in their own lives outside of work—and they are leaders within their areas of responsibility on the job. Every job and every role in an organization requires leadership. The truth of this becomes clear when you consider the fact that someone in a supervisory or management position can give orders, but if he or she is not trusted and respected as a true leader, employees will not provide their undivided support. Without the support of others, your ability to succeed is limited. This is why leadership is so powerful and necessary. Those who know how to lead don't have to threaten or bully others to achieve goals. Rather, effective leaders are masters of persuading, inspiring, coaxing, mentoring, and motivating. Effective leaders are successful because those who follow actually want to.

Not surprisingly, a key competency of effective leadership in any position or role within an organization is having a positive attitude. There are four reasons for this.

First, for most people, working is not what they would prefer to be doing. Recall back in Chapter 2 that we shared the results of research that showed only about 30 percent of employees and managers show up for work actively engaged and motivated to give 100 percent of their effort and creativity. The remaining 70 percent are coming to work "not engaged" or "actively disengaged." We think we can all agree that working around positive, motivated people is much more enjoyable than working around people who are depressed and negative.

Second, some coworkers have very difficult private lives away from the workplace. Your colleagues may be experiencing personal or family health issues, financial distress, behavioral problems with children, or many other challenges. Work can be a place where they have some respite to find positive people and forget some of their problems temporarily.

Third, research is clear that an employee's supervisor or manager is the most important relationship he or she has at work. A negative manager or supervisor can suck the life out of any work team. It is the manager's or supervisor's responsibility to build a positive work environment that brings out the best in everyone; this is also what employees expect from their superiors.

Finally, when you consider the facts, we typically spend almost half of our waking hours at work. Who wants to spend such a great amount of time in a negative, draining environment? Wouldn't you like to come to work every day to a place that is vibrant, creative, engaging, and motivating?

The bottom line is that working with a positive group can transform even relatively mundane jobs into positive and delightful experiences. Positive coworkers and management can inspire creativity, camaraderie, dedication, and productivity. Negative coworkers and management can make every day at work drag on interminably and decrease the employees' desire to help the organization succeed.

It's easy to observe positive or negative attitudes at work. For example, we recently read an article about a man named Ron who experienced poor customer service as a product of bad employee attitudes.[11] Ron had purchased a piece of electronic equipment. While trying to set up the equipment to get it to work, he ran into problems and called the company's customer service hotline for assistance. The first technician Ron talked with insisted that there was nothing wrong with the equipment and suggested that it must be Ron's fault. When Ron explained that everything in the network had worked perfectly until he powered up the new item, the technician laughed at him. Ron then asked to talk to his supervisor, and the technician told him to "get lost" (in stronger expletive terms) and hung up on Ron.

As bad as this example appears, remember that a positive attitude can offset a negative attitude and consider what happened next. Undeterred, Ron called back and spoke with a different technician, one who resolved the problem in a matter of minutes and then forwarded him to a supervisor. When Ron told the supervisor of his earlier experience, she asked Ron to give her one day to resolve the problem. She called back in less than fifteen minutes to tell Ron that she and the call center manager had reviewed the tape of the initial call, fired the first technician, and promoted the second one to a customer service training position. It went from being the worst customer service experience to one of the best in less than half an hour.

ATTITUDE AND CAREER SUCCESS

Garry and his colleague Dr. Gary Stroud were the keynote presenters at a Human Resources Association event. They were asked to speak on the topic, "Becoming a C-Suite Player in Your Profession." The "C-Suite" refers to the rarified corporate top echelon of any organization where the executives meet to set and implement strategy. The presentation was based on feedback provided by executives who identified what they were looking for in others to join their elite ranks.

The four qualities most desired were job competence, an understanding of the organization's business, the ability to work well with others, and a positive attitude. These may be qualities that senior executives in an organization say they are looking for at the top, but, if you think about it, these are also required qualities for anyone to get ahead in a career today.

First, regardless of the job you hold, you have to be competent at what you do. You likely will have attended a school or training program that prepared you for your work. However, in today's fast-moving world, you also need to stay abreast of changes in relevant issues facing your job, such as technology, procedures, competition, products, and services.

Second, you need to understand the business in which you work by knowing the answers to the following questions: What are the fundamental services or products your organization provides? Who are its primary customers and competitors? What makes you better or worse than your best competition? What can you do to help?

Third, in the "old days," a person could get by simply relying on his or her own technical skills. Today, most of us work in environments that require collaboration. This means that we need to have the skills to work well with others, including the ability to be a part of a well-functioning team. We need to know how to resolve conflict, communicate effectively, and adapt to differing personalities, cultures, and preferences.

Finally, you need to have a positive attitude. In today's rapidly changing working environment, we are inundated with change. Just about the time you learn a particular process, procedure, or software package, it changes. The ability to adapt and adjust to change is enhanced by a positive attitude.

In the work environment and in your personal life, it is your attitude that makes a tremendous difference. The ability to create and maintain healthy relationships among your management, coworkers, family members, and neighbors is a key to personal and organizational success.

WHAT HOLDS US BACK?

Knowing that a positive attitude is important to success in life and actually putting that knowledge into daily practice is easy for some and very difficult for others. In her book, *Feel the Fear and Do It Anyway*, best-selling author Susan Jeffers identifies a number of reasons why people have a hard time maintaining a positive attitude.[12] One of these reasons is the fear of failure; some people fear failure because they think they will not be good enough. The basis for this fear is that we feel unworthy compared to a false mental image of what constitutes perfection. By constantly comparing yourself against an imagined ideal of perfection, it is easy to become overwhelmed with self-judgment, which can take you on a downward mental and emotional spiral of unworthiness.[13]

Fear of the unknown is another reason that many people fear failure. In our hearts, we know that we can attain success only by taking action, but this very step often requires us to move into the unknown—and we all encounter those moments when moving forward fills us with fear.

The unknown can represent many things to different people. To some, the unknown represents not being sure of what we will encounter. To others, the unknown triggers our fear of not being in control. Also, the fear of the unknown may represent a lack of confidence in our own ability and resources. Frankly speaking, sometimes it is just easier to stay in the rut we are in rather than take positive action and initiative to take a risk.[14]

The media inundates us with unrealistic tales of individuals who appear to succeed at everything they attempt. The reality is that a lack of failure also equals a lack of

---

12   Jeffers, S. (1987). *Feel the Fear and Do It Anyway*. (1987). Toronto: Random House Publishing Group.

13   *Ibid.*

14   *Ibid.*

risk-taking. In order to do anything different, you have to take a risk. Arianna Huffington is the chair, president, and editor-in-chief of the Huffington Post Media Group, a nationally syndicated columnist, and author of thirteen books. In May 2005, she launched *The Huffington Post*, a news and blog site that quickly became one of the most widely read, linked-to, and frequently cited media brands on the Internet. In 2012, the site won a Pulitzer Prize for national reporting. In 2006, and again in 2011, she was named to the Time 100, *Time* magazine's list of the world's 100 most influential people. By most measures, one could say that Huffington has been quite successful, but she also observes that her success has not come without risk. In 2012, I had the pleasure of hearing her speak at a conference, where she said that she regularly reminds her daughters that failure is a stepping stone to success. "No one," she says, "succeeds without failing."[15]

You may have also seen the Oscar-winning movie Lincoln, which was released in 2012. Many of you may not be aware of the amazing challenges Abraham Lincoln faced throughout life. Consider the following: As a child, Lincoln's family's farm was destroyed by a flash flood. His mother died when he was nine. He ran for state legislature on several occasions—and lost. He was engaged to be married, but his fiancée died. He had periods of significant mental depression. He tried to become Speaker of the Legislature but was defeated. He was defeated in his first bid for a

15   Adrianna Huffington's Rule for Success: Dare to Fail. (2013). *Inc. Magazine*. Retrieved from www.inc.com/magazine/201302/rules-for-success/arianna-huffington-dare-to-fail.html

seat in the US Congress. He ran for the US Senate and lost. He eventually became President of the United States and is counted as one of the greatest presidents—if not the greatest—of all time.[16]

On the flip side of a fear of failure is a fear of success, which can also negatively affect a person's attitude. Psychologist Matina Horner first diagnosed the fear of success in the early 1970s. Her findings, especially as they related to fear of success in women at that time, were incredibly controversial. Since then, however, most scientists and psychologists agree that fear of success exists for both men and women.

Fear of success is similar to fear of failure because they have many of the same symptoms, and both fears hold you back from achieving your dreams and goals. You might wonder why someone would fear being successful. Dr. Horner has found that fear of success has several possible causes. We may fear what success will bring; for example, loneliness, new enemies, being isolated from our families, longer working hours, more criticism, or being asked for favors or money.

We may be afraid that the higher we climb in life, the farther we're going to fall when we make a mistake. Some people also fear that if they become successful, friends and family will react with jealousy and cynicism. And, finally, we may fear that accomplishing our goals and realizing that we have the power to be successful may actually cause intense regret about not acting sooner.[17]

16   Retrieved from www.abrahamlincolnonline.org/lincoln/education/failures.htm

17   Retrieved from https://sites.google.com/site/motivationataglanceischool/fear-of-success

HOW TO DEVELOP A POSITIVE ATTITUDE

Try this experiment. Hold up your thumb and forefinger about 2½ inches apart. Did you know that it takes about 1/100th of a second for Olympic sprinters to run that distance in a 100-meter race? [18] That can also be the difference between winning and losing. In the women's 100-meter dash at the 1992 Barcelona Olympic Games, for example, the American who won the gold medal crossed the finish line only 2½ inches in front of her closest opponent. Fifth place went to a Jamaican who finished a mere 6/100th of a second behind her. And yet that little bit of difference made all the difference in the world.

The same goes for attitude. As you have already learned in this chapter, research indicates that positive attitude can make all the difference in personal and professional success. So how do you build a positive attitude that helps you achieve greater levels of happiness, fulfillment, and success in life?

The first step is simply to recognize that you need to change your attitude. Most people can simply consider their own feelings about the world around them and determine if they have a positive or negative attitude. If you listen to yourself when in conversation with others, are you generally bemoaning how life is unfair? We all receive feedback in various forms from others that can suggest we are not projecting a positive attitude. Do other people avoid spending time with you? Perhaps it is because you bring them down. You might also consider with

18   Zimmerman, A. (2014). Cited in *Build A Positive Attitude With the Four-Day Attitude Diet.* Retrieved September 12, 2014, from http://sbinfocanada.about.com/od/motivation/a/posattitudeaz.htm

whom you tend to spend your time. Are they positive individuals or negative-minded people who regularly hold "pity parties" and lament the ills of the world. Finally, you might want to ask people whose opinion you respect for their views on how you project yourself to others.

If you determine that you can benefit from a change in how you view the world, the second step is to understand why this would be a good move. For example, many people find that a negative attitude toward life rarely leads to positive results (remember, we have already discussed that what you look for is what you tend to see). Some of the benefits of an attitude adjustment may be attracting more friends, putting yourself in a better position for a pay increase or a promotion, or simply feeling better about your life every day. Some people find it helpful to make a list of everything in their lives that matters to them and that brings them joy.

If you feel that a physical change would contribute to an attitude change, then start small. Pick one thing about yourself or your life that you would like to change and identify what you need to attain that goal. Perhaps you would feel better about yourself if you lost 20 pounds. Set a goal of losing a pound in the next two weeks, and then plan how you will walk a half mile or mile every day or eat a little less in one or more meals each day. Don't worry unnecessarily about setbacks and learn from your mistakes. Remember what Adrianna Huffington and Sir Richard Branson said earlier, mistakes are simply part of the path to success.

ATTITUDE TIPS FROM PANDA

With very few exceptions, Panda is delighted to see Garry and the rest of the family in the morning and when they come home, as well as to greet any visitor to their home. Panda's disposition and attitude is always upbeat. Studies on which companies are most successful show that those with the best customer service are more profitable and survive

Personal Activity 2:

WHAT WOULD YOU LIKE TO CHANGE?

Start now: think of something that you want to change; think positively about how and why it is something you want to change. Try to recall when this item started and how it got out of control. How do you want to take ownership of the power to change it?

Write the steps you think you need to take right now to facilitate the change you want to make.

Notes:

when times are tough. And what's a huge component of good customer service? An attitude like Panda's: friendly, welcoming, and happy to interact with each new person. As consumers, we have a choice about where we shop, and we are mostly likely to shop where we have good customer experiences.

The same is true for university faculty. We have to make choices about which textbooks to order for our classes. There are a number of textbook companies that send their representatives to meet with us on a fairly regular basis to discuss upcoming courses and to inform us about why we should select their textbooks on particular topics. Many of the staff members where we work tend to gravitate toward textbooks published by a specific textbook vendor. Let us stress that the level of support, quality of instructional materials, and content are fairly even across most publishers. The reason so many faculty members select their textbooks from this particular vendor is because the customer service representative, Rhonda, is the best! She is vivacious, open, funny, and sincerely interested in each and every faculty member. When Rhonda is in the building, faculty who hear her voice get up from their desks and find her to say hello and catch up on how she and her family are doing.

Rhonda's disposition is not a facade; it is how she is. She is an expert in her field; she knows the textbooks backward and forward. She understands her competition

and knows what services and support her company provides that differentiate it from the competition. She gets along wonderfully with anybody; it does not matter what discipline a faculty member represents.

Now, the customer service representatives from competing publishers are also experts on their products and very competent in the field. The difference is that Rhonda has the best attitude, and it comes across loud and clear.

We realize that some readers are thinking, "No, she is just very good at putting on an act." First, that is negative thinking. Second, as researchers, we faculty members are very adept at spotting a snow job. Rhonda is truly excited to see each of us and chat about our professional and personal endeavors. She really does enjoy hearing about each person's plans for improving his or her classes or integrating new technology to engage students. Like Panda, she is not afraid to let people know how much she enjoys her job and how enthusiastic she is to spend time with them.

Another example comes from Dr. John Izzo, bestselling author of *The Five Secrets You Must Discover Before You Die*. Dr. Izzo relates that a friend told him about a housekeeper he met at one of the Disney-based hotels. As he went down the hall, he noticed her arranging the stuffed animals on a bed. When he asked what she was doing, she told him that when a family left stuffed animals in the room, she liked to arrange the animals doing different things. That particular day she had arranged them around a book as if they were reading stories to each other. "When the family comes back," she said, "they will be filled with smiles." She smiled herself and continued, "Tomorrow, I will arrange the stuffed animals as if they are playing cards."[19] You get the picture: every day, the housekeeper was looking for new ways to thrill the people who were staying at the hotel.

Shouldn't that be the lesson we all learn from dogs? Greet every day for what it is: an opportunity to make a difference in your life and in the lives of others. We have tried to learn from our dogs that while we cannot always choose what happens to us, we can always choose what happens within us and how we respond to what happens.

Some things in life are beyond our control. Most things, however, we can influence. My attitude about the areas beyond my control and within my control makes a great difference in how I approach life and the influence I have on my colleagues and family. Your attitude makes a difference in your life, too. Make sure it is a positive attitude that makes a positive difference.

---

19   Izzo, J. (2004). *Second Innocence*. San Francisco, CA: Berrett-Koehler Publishers, p. 86.

How you interact with others can have a large effect on how you feel. Dogs greet each day with vibrant and clear enthusiasm. What can you do to modify your morning routine so that you start each day with a joyous and positive outlook?

Embracing your life experiences—even the ones that were painful or embarrassing—is an important characteristic of a good attitude. We often fret and worry over things that happened in the past that really did not amount to much in the big scheme of our lives. Take a moment to remember a couple of bad things that have happened to you in the past. List these in the space below.

Now, make a list of what you gained from the experience(s) you listed in question 2. What did you learn? How have you become a better person, and how have you grown?

Flip side exercise: Most problems we encounter in life have a flip side, or humorous side, to them. For example, on the next page, you will see a problem situation and then the flip side of looking at that problem which, while acknowledging the reality of the situation, also provides a means for reducing stress, tension, and other negative feelings.

SITUATION	FLIP SIDE
You got a dent in your new car	Throw a party to celebrate not having to worry about the first dent
You miss your connection flight home	View the time as an opportunity to explore the airport shops and people-watch

Share your positive attitude with others. As we've suggested in this chapter, we like dogs because they have and share such a positive attitude. The good news is that we can, too! The following are a number of ways in which you can share your positive attitude with others. Pick two or three that fit your style and/or add your own to the bottom of the list. Remember, the more you share your positive attitude with others, the more positive your attitude will remain.

* Be more positive around my family and/or coworkers.
* Share my sense of humor by telling appropriate jokes or humorous views on life situations.
* Communicate my positive attitude by focusing conversations on the positive and rewarding aspects of life, work, and relationships instead of joining in on negative gossip.
* Brighten someone else's day with a token such as a flower, candy bar, smiley sticker, or something similar.
* Go out of my way to visit others who are having trouble in life and seek opportunities to help where appropriate.
* Transmit my positive attitude to anyone I talk to on the phone.

Add your own opportunity for sharing your positive attitude:

CHAPTER 7
WORK–LIFE BALANCE

*Dogs are our link
to paradise. They don't know
evil or jealousy or discontent.
To sit with a dog on a hillside
on a glorious afternoon is to be
back in Eden, where doing nothing
was not boring—it was peace.*

—MILAN KUNDERA

One of the benefits of our work as university professors is the opportunity to visit many different organizations and talk to people in a range of roles: janitors, accountants, human resources managers, engineers, administrative assistants, executives, and so on. When we ask them to pinpoint what they struggle with most at home and work, more often than not they identify work—life balance.

Work—life balance has become an increasing problem over the past few decades in most developed countries. Organizations and employees are under constant pressure to adapt to changing customer demands, the need for quality products and services, and cutthroat competition. The good news is that most employees and management have taken the challenge to heart and are working longer hours to help their organizations succeed. The bad news is that in a constant effort to "do more with less," managers and employees are spreading themselves too thin and losing touch with important aspects of their lives. We see this in the lives of professionals who are successful financially but whose personal and family lives are in serious turmoil.

We find that paying attention to our dogs helps ground us and serves as a reminder about what is important. Karen Hough, founder and CEO of ImprovEdge, shared a wonderful story about how her dog, Valoche, helped her find balance. In addition to running a thriving training and consulting business, Karen is also the bestselling author of *The Improvisation Edge: Secrets to Building Trust and Radical Collaboration at Work*, recipient of the International Silver Stevie Award for Most Innovative Company of the Year 2012, and winner of the ATHENAPowerLink Award for Outstanding Woman-Owned Business. When Garry asked Karen if she could share her experience and perspective on the value of work–life balance, she said, "Yes, but I should also be clear that living a balanced life is something that has not come easy. In my mid-twenties, I had no concept of work–life balance. I was lucky to have a great acting career in Chicago, so I had shows and rehearsals every day and most nights of the week. In addition, an actor must audition constantly, since our work might only last one day (shooting a commercial) or a few months (a run of a live show). Even though my career supported me, I also had huge student loans, so I filled in every spare minute with temp jobs, waitressing jobs—anything flexible and part-time."

Karen hesitated and then went on. "I told myself that it was all necessary, but I was honestly running away. The tragic loss of a sister, a grandfather, [and] an uncle and the heartbreaking end of a romance felt unbearable. I found that if I stayed exhausted, I slept without dreaming. And my dreams were rarely good."

One night, Karen was driving a friend home after a late-night movie. It was dark and storming, with limited visibility. Suddenly, her passenger screamed, "Stop!" just in time to keep Karen from hitting a dog standing in the street. Karen and her friend got out of the car to find a bedraggled, abandoned mutt who gratefully licked her hand as she brought him into the car. The dog, who she named Valoche, had found a home, and Karen's life changed.

"I had to find an apartment that would accept a dog," she said, "and I had to take care of someone who would not put up with my ridiculous hours and a lack of attention. I had to think about exercising Valoche, his health [and] personal welfare, and getting him trained." Karen also found that although caring for Valoche took time and attention, she was also beginning to eliminate things that drained her. "Valoche was filling me with the warmth of his devotion and a sense of responsibility. And, importantly, he was also filling those dark, empty places of grief that existed inside of me. Valoche was the only man in my life for over a year, and our relationship prompted me to reassess some friendships that were not healthy, realign my career to be more meaningful, and remember to take care of myself."

Karen and Valoche's story does not end there. A few months after Valoche came home with Karen, she got up one morning and threw on some sweats to take Valoche to Dog Beach on Lake Michigan. She was surprised by a purebred Labrador who ran up to her dog and began playing. The owner of the Lab was even more surprised, because the dog was normally perfectly behaved, but she had broken away from her owner the moment she saw Valoche.

Karen smiles as she described the scene: "The dogs hit it off, and so did we. But while we were busy talking, the two dogs rolled in dead fish that had washed up on the shore. To put it mildly, the two dogs were disgusting. My new acquaintance, Todd, suggested we walk to a nearby self-serve dog wash, and it was only after we had washed our dogs that I realized I had not brought my wallet. Todd gallantly paid, so I asked him to come see my show that night. I promised to leave two tickets at the door, and although he told me he only needed one, I insisted on leaving two (I really wanted to make sure this guy was single). He came alone and sat in the front row, and I was a goner. Thirteen months later, walking those two dogs in the evening on Dog Beach, he proposed."

Karen notes that she and Todd have now been married for eighteen years, lived in seven homes, reared three children, and had only one other dog since the original two. She says, "We keep crazy schedules at times, but as long as there is a dog in the house, it reminds us of how lucky we are to be together and how very critical it is to take a walk, play outside, calm down, and find balance."[1]

WHAT IS WORK–LIFE BALANCE?

As Karen's story suggests, in a world filled with conflicting demands, responsibilities, and commitments, finding balance in our lives is often very difficult. One of the reasons attaining balance may be elusive is that, despite the fact that work–life balance has been studied formally since the 1930s, there are many different definitions. The definition we like best was on Wikipedia, "Work–life balance is a concept including proper prioritizing between 'work' (career and ambition) and 'lifestyle' (health, pleasure, leisure, family, and spiritual development/meditation)."[2] Of all the definitions we reviewed, this one seemed to sum up the main elements of balance in terms most of us would recognize.

---

1   Interview with Karen Hough, February 2013.
2   Retrieved July 30, 2015, from https://en.wikipedia.org/wiki/Work%E2%80%93life_balance

Dogs seem to be particularly adept at living balanced lives. Panda has what appears to be a wonderful sense of transitioning between the major aspects of his life, whether sleeping, resting, playing, or eating. (Garry's son, Ian, would also argue that barking at big trucks or people who come to the door is also a major aspect of Panda's life, so we'll add "protecting the homestead" to the list.)

Panda seems to have set times of the day when he transitions from one of these life tasks to another, but he is also able to adapt quickly. For example, if he is resting, and someone wants to throw the ball, he quickly gets into play mode. But after a rigorous bout of chasing the ball, he shifts smoothly back to rest mode again. And, from what we can tell, Panda and every other dog in the world can quickly switch from whatever they are doing to "stop-and-eat something" mode.

Even though most people would agree with the Wikipedia definition of work–life balance, many still have a hard time achieving it. One factor that may inhibit us from achieving a greater level of balance was identified by Nancy Lockwood with the Society for Human Resources Management in an article titled "Work-Life Balance: Challenges and Solutions."[3] Nancy points out that when someone left work twenty or thirty years ago, he or she could not check in via laptop or cell phone, and it was very difficult for someone at the office to connect with that person. Today, many people do not "turn off" work at all. Researchers call this "cognitive intrusion of work." Because we are always connected to work, our

---

3   Lockwood, N. (2003). Work/Life Balance: Opportunities and Solutions. *SHRM Research Quarterly*. Retrieved November 12, 2014.

family, our friends, and the larger world through our smart devices, we do not have the cognitive (or thinking) space needed to process, organize, and respond to the challenges of life in a complex society. In essence, we do not have the downtime needed to relax, think about what is important, and act accordingly.

WHY IS WORK–LIFE BALANCE A PROBLEM?

The paradox of our lives is that even though we are inundated with information and electronic demands, we also report that we are less willing to put personal and family lives on hold for work. For example, a study by the consulting firm Accenture revealed that more than half of men and women surveyed said that work–life balance was a key indicator of whether or not they had successful careers, and they ranked work–life balance ahead of money, recognition, and autonomy.[4] In fact, according to Accenture, work–life balance is so important that more than half of those surveyed have turned down job offers because of the potential negative impact on their life priorities. Clearly, balance is and will continue to be a very important aspect of employees' expectations for their work environment. This is in direct contradiction to the fact that many organizations expect employees to put work first, ahead of personal and family lives. Not surprisingly, the gulf between the two can lead to a host of problems for both individuals and organizations.[5]

4   Retrieved from www.businessnewsdaily.com/4049-employees-want-work-life-balance.html
5   *Ibid.*

On a personal level, living a life that is not balanced leads to a variety of issues that can affect the health and well-being of relationships. Furthermore, studies suggest that not paying attention to what you feel is most important can lead to depression, alcohol and drug problems, compulsive eating, and anger issues.

When employees struggle with balance issues at work, organizations also feel the effects. A study by the Society for Human Resources Management observes that poor work–life balance can lead to increasing levels of employee stress, low employee morale, increased use of sick time, distrust, embezzlement, task avoidance, turnover, and poor productivity.[6] These trends are also true outside the United States. Research conducted in the United Kingdom shows that the pressure of increasingly demanding work expectations is perhaps the biggest and most pressing challenge to the mental health of the country's general population. The struggle for work–life balance has escalated to a point in Japan that they have a word—*karoshi*—that translates as "death from overwork" to describe the increasing numbers of executives, managers, and employees who died suddenly while still in their prime years and with no previous sign of illness.[7]

6   Lockwood, N. R. (2003). WorkLife Balance, Challenges and Solutions. Society for Human Resource Management, Quarterly Research.

7   Death by Overwork in Japan. (2007, December 19). *The Economist.* Retrieved July 21, 2015, from www.economist.com/node/10329261

WHAT WORK–LIFE BALANCE IS *NOT*

Now that you have a good idea of what work–life-balance is and how it can affect your personal, professional, and family life, let's look at what work–life balance is *not*. First, balance is not a state of nirvana in which everything is perfect every day for the rest of your life. Although Panda and his doggy friends have great lives, they are certainly not perfect. Dogs fight with each other, misbehave, become ill, and get hurt. Our lives have challenges, too. We have problems with others at home and work, we become ill or injured, and, like the saying goes, "stuff happens," and things do not turn out as we planned. One of the differences between humans and dogs is that they don't appear to dwell on misfortune; they experience it for what it is and move on with the expectation that things will get better.

Second, living a balanced life does not mean devoting the same amount of time and deliberation to every aspect of your life on a daily basis. In today's fast-paced world, it has become a way of life for people to attempt to pay attention to everything at once. This way of life has become so pervasive that we have a name for it: multitasking. We know many parents who pursue the ideal of "super-mom"

Personal Activity:

BARRIERS TO WORK-LIFE BALANCE

What forces or influences in your life keep you from living the balanced life you desire?

Notes:

and "super-dad" by fulfilling their parental roles, working full time, and living highly engaging social and community lives. Don't you love those commercials on television that depict mom or dad on the phone with the office, skillfully solving major problems at work while cooking a meal, mopping up spilled milk, doing a load of laundry, and getting kids dressed to catch the school bus? We know this is not possible.

Psychology professor Dr. Russell Poldrack of the University of California, says that human beings are not wired to multitask.[8] "We are really built to focus," he says, "and when we force ourselves to multitask, we're driving ourselves to perhaps be less efficient in the long run even though it sometimes feels like we're being more efficient."[9] On the contrary, one of the qualities we admire about dogs is that when they are with you, they are with you. They focus on one thing at a time. In life, we need to learn to focus our attention on what is most important at that moment. When at home, focus on your family, not on work. And when you are at work and in the middle of an important task, focus on that task, not what you are planning for the weekend at home.

8   Retrieved from www.thestar.com/life/health_wellness/diseases_cures/2008/07/02/can_you_finish_this_story_without_being_interrupted.html

9   Ibid.

Third, work–life balance is not measured by how much money you make or how much "stuff" you have accumulated. We live in a culture that suggests that happiness and wealth go hand in hand. Marketers work nonstop to convince us that if we just have more of whatever they are trying to sell, we will "have it made." But accumulating more is not the goal of life. Nobody on his or her deathbed wishes that he or she had a bigger car, more jewelry, a grander home, or more money. This point is made clear when you consider the man in a retirement home who belatedly recognized this, saying, "I wish I had paid more attention to people instead of making money. The BMW I worked so hard to own never comes to visit."

This observation is pertinent to each of us because when you get to the end of your life, it will not be how much money you made or what you accrued that matters, it will be the lives you touched in a positive way, the adventures in which you participated, and the days you played with others. Dogs remind us that the most important part of every day is spending time with the people they love. As the great American humorist Will Rogers said, "No man can be condemned for owning a dog. As long as he has a dog, he has a friend; and the poorer he gets, the better friend he has."[10]

Fourth, work–life balance is not the same for everyone. We are all individuals, and our capacities for work, our interests, and our circumstances all vary considerably. This is true for dogs, too. Every dog we meet has a different personality, and this is also true of human beings. Some of us are extroverts who find balance in crowds of people. Others are introverts who need time alone. The job that one person does every day may be far more engaging and rewarding than the job of another person. One person may find that hiking through the mountains is wonderfully relaxing, while another may find the same level of joy in reading a book or cooking a gourmet meal. We think that recognizing and affirming that we are all different helps us understand that the path we take to achieve balance will probably be different from that of other people.

FINDING WORK–LIFE BALANCE

It is tempting to believe that we would find greater balance in our lives if, like our pet dogs, we had someone else providing for all our needs and all we had to do is lie around, play, and scratch ourselves occasionally. Yes, it's tempting, but it's also

---

10   Retrieved June 10, 2015, from www.willrogers.com/quotes.html

inaccurate. Did you know that while most people say that they would retire if they won a huge lottery, research among those who actually did hit the jackpot indicates that most continue working?[11] Research conducted by Dr. Scott Highhouse, a psychology professor at Bowling Green State University, indicates that of 185 lottery winners, 63 percent continued working at the same company, 10 percent started their own businesses, and 11 percent cut back to part-time work. This means that after winning a huge amount of money, 84 percent of new millionaires continued to work! Dr. Highhouse interprets these results in the following way: "Certainly, money is important, but there are a lot of other aspects to work that play a big role, including relationships, achievement needs that people have, and status needs that go beyond money."[12]

These findings suggest that becoming fabulously wealthy is not the ticket to balance that many of us think it would be. That said, suppose we asked you to take a minute to consider what is most important in your life. What would you say? Is it your IRA, car, stereo, cell phone, home, or jewelry? We suspect that while you might identify these things as nice to have, they are not the most important

11   Powerball Numbers: Why Do Lottery Winners Keep on Working? (2011, June 2). *The Christian Science Monitor*. Retrieved from www.csmonitor.com/Business/new-economy/2011/0602/Powerball-numbers-Why-do-lottery-winners-keep-working

12   *Ibid.*

elements in your life. Rather, there are more important aspects to life, such as working to make a difference in your life and the lives of others; creating and sustaining healthy, vibrant relationships with others; and experiencing joy. These factors are interesting because we also believe that people like dogs for the same reasons: they do make a difference in our lives; we do have great relationships with our dogs, and we do find joy in their unabashed pleasure in life and our company. How do we attain a greater sense of satisfaction and balance?

PURPOSE

Mark Twain said, "The two most important days in your life are the day you are born and the day you find out why."[13] You may know some people who seem to be going through life with meaning, purpose, and joy. In our experience, dogs certainly understand their purpose in life as expressed by Steve Grill, the general manager for LA Fitness in New Albany, Ohio. Grill said, "Dogs don't just think they are man's best friend. They think they are your only friend!"

13   Retrieved June 10, 2015, from www.brainyquote.com/quotes/authors/m/mark_twain.html

In his book, *Five Secrets You Must Discover Before You Die*, Dr. John Izzo relates that to live a life of purpose is to live with intention. Living with intention, or purpose, is a lifelong effort to live in honest awareness of who you are and what special gifts are yours to share with the world as well as the willingness to reflect often and critically to determine if you are on the right path. This is no small requirement because it is easy to live a life in which we do not know who we are or what we have to contribute. Some people simply go through life as it comes and rarely, if ever, make any attempt to determine what impact their behavior and actions are having on themselves, their family members, their coworkers, and their community. Dr. Izzo suggests that the first step in determining your purpose is to ask yourself three questions:

- Am I following my heart and being true to myself?
- Is my life focused on things that really matter to me?
- Am I being the person I want to be in the world?[14]

Answering these three questions will help you clarify your real strengths and connect to your personal creative capacities so you can share the best that you have to offer with the world.

14   Izzo, J. (2008). *The Five Secrets You Must Discover Before You Die*. San Francisco, CA: Berrett-Koehler Publishers.

Thankfully, it is never too late to find your purpose. Ken Robinson tells the wonderful story of a literary editor he worked with on a book he had written. One day, when they were talking about writing, she revealed that she had spent several years as a concert pianist before becoming a literary editor. She explained that one day she had given a concert in London with a distinguished conductor. After the event, they were having dinner together, and the conductor mentioned how well she had played, adding, "But you didn't enjoy it, did you?" She was taken aback by his question, but after thinking for a moment, she agreed that she rarely enjoyed playing the piano. He then asked why she did it, and she replied, "Because I am good at it."[15]

She explained that she had been born into a musical family, taken lessons, and showed talent. She pursued music in college and eventually began a career as a concert pianist. Neither she nor anyone else had ever stopped to ask if she enjoyed what she was doing. When she finished her story, the conductor said, "Being good at something isn't a good enough reason to spend your life doing it." In the weeks that followed, she reflected on what he had said and concluded that the conductor was right. To her credit, she finished the season of concerts and then turned to books, an art form she really loved and in which she also excelled.[16]

LIVE IN THE MOMENT

Do you ever find yourself sitting in an important meeting at work but thinking about what you are going to do the coming weekend? Or maybe you are "listening" to a loved one telling you about his or her day while you are really thinking about some project at work? How many times have you found yourself on vacation in a wonderful location but unable to relax and enjoy yourself for worrying about something going on at work? Why can't we just enjoy the moment we inhabit?

A very talented associate of ours, Kelly Gurnett, summed up this dilemma, saying, "If I could learn to be half as present and joyful as my little dog when she's tearing the fluff out of her favorite toy, I would be a happy person indeed." Isn't that the truth? Our dogs never fail to remind us through their behavior that if something is worth doing, it is worth doing with your whole being. Most of us live our lives in the past or future and miss out on the present, and it's easy to see

---

15   Retrieved June 10, 2015, from www.ted.com/talks/ken_robinson_says_schools_kill_creativity?language=en
16   Ibid.

why this is the case. As we noted previously, we live in a world that contributes to mental fragmentation; we are bombarded by media and social messages that encourage us to dwell on what we have done wrong in the past and how inadequate we are in the present (looks, weight, sexual attractiveness, wealth), or to worry ourselves sick about what may or may not happen in the future. The Buddhists call these our "monkey thoughts" because they are thoughts that race about in our minds just like monkeys swinging from one tree to another.[17]

The problem is that the present moment is the only place we can exist. We should plan for the future and we often desire things we don't have, but we can only find balance and happiness in the here and now. Consider how we admire the ability of dogs to live in the present. As mentioned, when a dog is with you, he is with you. When a dog is playing, he is really playing. Dogs embody the saying "yesterday is history, tomorrow is a mystery, today is a gift, and that is why it is called the present."[18]

GIVE MORE THAN YOU TAKE

Dogs definitely give more than they take. Conversely, we human beings are so competitive in our orientation to others. As suggested previously, it may be in part due to our upbringing and the constant "what's in it for me" mentality fostered through the media. For most of us, the world is a limited set of resources and opportunities. If I give more or you get more, then there is less for me. You have been taught since you were a child that if you worked hard enough, put in enough hours, and clawed your way to the top, then you would be happy. But face it—this is simply not true. We have both worked with a number of very wealthy individuals who lived profoundly unhappy and imbalanced lives. These individuals spent their entire careers scrambling to climb the corporate ladder and amass fortunes and accolades only to find their lives very empty of substantive relationships, love, and a feeling of contribution.

Dogs, and the happiest, most balanced people in the world, understand that you can give all the love, forgiveness, and positive feelings you want, and you will still have infinitely more to give. You can love your spouse, mother, father, brother,

---

17   Is a Monkey Mind Robbing You of Your Peace and Serenity? (n.d.). Retrieved April 3, 2015, from www.find-happiness. com/monkey-mind.html

18   Retrieved July 8, 2015, from https://answers.yahoo.com/question/index?qid= 20071130182336AA7qVmv

sister, other relatives, friends, and on and on and still have all the love in the world to give to others. Your "warehouse" of available love is not diminished in any way.

Albert Einstein recognized the value of giving more than you take when he said, "The value of a man resides in what he gives and not in what he is capable of receiving."[19] All of the great models of history—Gandhi, Mother Teresa, Martin Luther King, Nelson Mandela, and others—stressed the importance and value of being selfless in service to others. They stressed the value of giving freely of your personal time, wisdom, and expertise by volunteering to do charitable service outside your immediate community as well. Giving back will not only make you better as a person, they say, but it will also help others.

LIVE LIFE FULLY

A number of books have been written that profile the responses shared by elderly individuals when asked what they regret most in their lives. By far, the most common response is that they did not take more risks and live life more fully. Reflect on this for a moment. These individuals did not regret the risks they did take in life; instead, they wish they had risked even more! Like many of us, these individuals report that they passed up opportunities to enjoy life more fully because they succumbed to the fears that hold many of us back. One of the reasons people avoid trying something new is the fear of making a mistake. They report, "I might do something wrong and look silly." Yes, but who cares? When we think of

19   Retrieved June 10, 2015, from http://thinkexist.com/quotation/the_value_of_a_man_resides_in_what_he_gives_and/15612.html

all the things we have done that really were wrong and silly, most honestly do not amount to much in hindsight.

Another reason people avoid living life fully is because it means getting out of the comfortable rut in which they exist. Garry recently talked with a colleague who had been invited to go to China to speak at a conference. His wife could have traveled with him, but she refused to go along. When Garry asked why, his colleague said, "Well, she said she did not want to go because she thought the people would be different and she might not like the food." While Garry did not say this out loud, he was thinking, "Wow, those are the exact reasons my wife and I love to travel!" We enjoy meeting diverse people, staying in unique locations, eating food we never see in the United States, visiting interesting places, and experiencing new cultures and practices that differ from our own.

Fortunately, living life fully does not mean you have to go around the world. The elderly people interviewed said they wish they had traveled more within their own communities, states, or regions. Some wished they had read more books, eaten different items when they went out to eat (instead of the same thing every time), learned to play an instrument, gone back to school for a different degree, changed jobs to something for which they had a true passion (even though it paid less), or tried out for the community choir or stage production.

Dogs absolutely live life to the fullest. When we come home from the store, Panda is curious about every item we pull out of the grocery bag. If you hold a can of beans, a package of frozen shrimp, or a bunch of bananas down for his inspection, he will sniff and lick every one of them. He loves going to new parks and exploring. He appears to live life with the gusto recommended by motivational speaker Anthony Robbins: "Live life fully while you're here. Experience everything. Take care of yourself and your friends. Have fun, be crazy, be weird. Go out and screw up! You're going to anyway, so you might as well enjoy the process. Take the opportunity to learn from your mistakes; find the cause of your problem and eliminate it. Don't try to be perfect; just be an excellent example of being human."[20]

The lesson shared by those wise elderly men and women nearing the end of their lives is easily overlooked. When we are young, we think we have all the time in the world. We put things off, saying "someday I will." I will try skydiving, I will write a poem, I will take time to go to my kid's baseball game, I will visit the Grand Canyon, I will learn a new language, and so on. But days come and go, and we never do what we desire. We fail to take risks and live life as fully as we hoped, and then, suddenly, the kids are grown and our health has declined. The great poet Henry David Thoreau said, "Oh God! To reach the point of death only to realize you have never lived."[21] The time to live fully is now, not ten or twenty years in the future.

In his marvelous book, *Living, Loving & Learning*, Leo Buscaglia describes a letter written by an eighty-five-year old man in the *Journal of Humanistic Psychology*. The man

20   Robbins, A. (2015). Retrieved from www.values.com/inspirational-quotes/5463-live-life-fully-while-youre-here-experience

21   Retrieved from http://en.wikiquote.org/wiki/Henry_David_Thoreau

says in the letter, "If I had my life to live over again, I'd try to make more mistakes next time. I wouldn't try to be so perfect. I would relax more. I'd limber up. I'd be sillier than I've been on this trip. In fact, I know very few things I would take so seriously. I'd be crazier. I'd take more chances, I'd take more trips, I'd climb more mountains, I'd swim more rivers, I'd watch more sunsets, I'd go more places I've never been to. I'd eat more ice cream and fewer beans." He ends with the following: "If I had to do it all over again, I'd start barefoot earlier in the spring and stay that way later in the fall. I'd ride more merry-go-rounds, I'd watch more sunrises, and I'd play with more children if I had my life to live over again. But, you see, I don't."[22] Neither do you and I.

Garry recalls that his mixed-up priorities caused unnecessary turmoil in his life. When Garry was in his late twenties and early thirties, he remembers working in a high-technology environment that was very fast-paced and very exciting. Garry reminiscences, "I enjoyed the people I worked with and the work I was accomplishing, and I was well paid. However, I also found that I enjoyed the constant excitement and adrenaline rush of work far more than the humdrum of my home life. At work, I was solving problems, I was making a difference for the company, and (in my mind) I was demonstrating my prowess as a provider for my family. My life had become one in which work took the forefront and family a distant second. In hindsight, I can see why this would occur. After an exhilarating day at work, it was a letdown to go home, where a stressed wife, crying children, and mundane tasks awaited me. So, like many other well-intended workaholics, I began to turn inward, thinking, 'Why doesn't my family appreciate and understand

how hard I am working to provide them a great life?' I was like a very happy hamster on a wheel; I was running very fast, chasing external rewards, and going nowhere.

"Not surprisingly, my negative attitude,

22   Buscaglia, L. (1983). *Living, Loving and Learning*. New York: Ballantine Books.

misguided priorities, and resentment began to wear on my marriage. Then, one day, the company decided to downsize. While I was not among those let go, I was stunned to see highly competent associates who had given decades of their minds, bodies, and souls to the organization being walked out the door by security at the same time senior executives lavished raises and bonuses on themselves. It was a gut-wrenching experience and the kick in the head I needed to refocus on what was truly important in my life: my family and my health. So I stepped off the hamster wheel to reconnect with my wife and children."

Sometimes, when we observe dogs, we think they must know that we each of us has only so much time on this earth and that it is up to us to ensure that we live balanced lives. Focusing on our purpose, living for the moment, giving more than we take, and living fully in all aspects of our lives is not trivial; it's sanity. We are not naive enough to think that there are no more late nights at work or crazy deadlines in our futures. One thing we have learned is that, no matter the job, there will always be more work, emails, and meetings. Panda, Skeeter, Domino, Spot, Pup, and all the dogs we have known have taught us that it is important to rest, to play, to explore, to lay in the sunshine, and to scratch. Oh, yeah, and always make time for those you love. That's work–life balance.

Thinking about Work-Life Balance

In the normal course of our lives, we can't help but observe that change is a natural part of our environment. Summer gives way to fall, which is followed by winter and then spring. People grow, have families, go to school, get jobs, retire, and ultimately pass on. Making improvements in our lives means taking time to plan and design the lives we want. In the following table, consider several major life categories and conduct a "gap analysis" to determine where you are now versus where you want to go.

LIFE CATEGORY	WHERE ARE YOU NOW?	WHAT DO YOU REALLY WANT?
Family		
Spiritual		
Social		
Health		
Work		
Personal		
Education		
Other		

When you are successful, what difference will it make in your life and the lives of others?

Now that you have a better idea of where you are now and where you want to go, the next step is to develop an action plan for attaining the life balance you desire. Look over the following table and identify one area in each category that you want to improve upon.

LIFE CATEGORY	WHAT DO YOU NEED TO STOP DOING?	WHAT DO YOU NEED TO START DOING?	WHEN ARE YOU GOING TO START?	HOW WILL YOU KNOW WHEN YOU ARE SUCCESSFUL?
Family				
Spiritual				
Social				
Health				
Work				
Personal				
Education				
Other				

CONCLUSION

*Thorns may hurt you,
men desert you, sunlight
turn to fog; but you're
never friendless ever,
if you have a dog.*

—Douglas Mallock

*B*uck Bresler, Garry's father-in-law, owns a magic shop in Cleveland, Ohio, and is a very accomplished magician in his own right. One of the more popular tricks he sells is the Chinese locking rings. You have probably seen this trick before, where a magician holds up two or more separate metal rings and then appears to magically link them all together. In this book, we have talked about each of the seven secrets of happy dogs as if, like the Chinese locking rings at the beginning of the magic trick, each habit were separate. In reality, we believe the seven secrets of happiness—loyalty, communication, play, unconditional love, forgiveness, a positive attitude, and balance—are highly interconnected with each other, like the locking rings at the end of the magic trick. We admire these qualities in dogs; dogs appear to incorporate all seven into their lives at all times.

We began this book by asking a series of simple questions. What difference would it make in your life if you took greater care to communicate effectively with others and to really listen instead of focusing solely on getting your point across? Suppose you tried harder to consider the needs of others or to honestly demonstrate greater loyalty to your family, friends, and colleagues? How would your life change for the better if you harbored fewer grudges against others, if you stepped out of your comfort zone and experienced more of life, if you loved others unconditionally, if you went through life with a more positive attitude, if you felt a great sense of work–life balance? Would your life be better? We think most of us know in our hearts that the answer is yes.

Of course, knowing our lives would be better if we change is easier said than done. We find that, in our own lives and in the lives of those who attend our speaking or training engagements, overcoming one's own internal inertia is a major stumbling block. While we hope you feel good and have enjoyed the book, and we recognize that it is nice that you now know the seven secrets of happiness as embodied by dogs, they will remain abstract principles until you begin to live them in your life—until you put these secrets into practice.

The challenge of change reminds us of the story about how some native tribes catch monkeys.[1] In certain parts of the world, the local populations catch monkeys

1   Collier, N. (2007). The Monkey's Fist: An Ancient Parable for Modern Times. NSC Blog. Retrieved July 21, 2015, from http://www.nscblog.com/miscellaneous/the-monkeys-fist-an-ancient-parable-for-modern-times/

as pets or to sell to zoos. The manner in which they catch monkeys without hurting them is quite ingenious. The locals drill a hole into the side of a coconut; the hole is just big enough for a monkey to stick its hand in, and the coconut is secured to a tree with a length of chain. They then place some seeds, rice, or bananas inside the coconut and walk away. Sooner or later, a monkey comes along and reaches inside the coconut to grab the food. The monkey quickly discovers that while its hand is small enough to reach into the coconut, it is too big to pull out with a fistful of food. Caught by its own hand, the monkey pulls and squirms but does not release the food, which would ensure its freedom. Later, the natives return and collect the healthy, but angry, monkey.

While we humans don't trap ourselves by sticking our hands inside coconuts, we do trap ourselves in ways of thinking and behaving that are not productive and keep us from attaining the level of joy and happiness we could experience in life. We know we should embrace change, and yet we still refuse to let go of what is familiar.

So our question to you is this: What do you have firmly grasped in your hand in the coconut trap of your own creation? Is it an unhealthy lifestyle? Are you harboring grudges that have been eating away at you for years and should be forgiven? Are you failing to take time to focus on those who love you and desire more of your attention? The bottom line is that if you find yourself trapped by a behavior or an outmoded way of thinking or perceiving, then, unlike the monkey, you have the ability to step back, look critically at what is going on, swallow your pride, and do something about it. As human beings, we have the capacity to open our hands and let go of what is holding us back in life.

Our hope is that you have come to see yourself and your relationships with others in a new way. Since we began writing this book, there have been many occasions upon which we found ourselves beginning to think negatively or reacting to pressure at home or at work by snapping at someone. When this occurred, we found it very helpful to have something on hand that reminds us about our purpose in life and how we hope to relate to others. As Garry reflects, it may sound a bit corny, but he has a picture of Panda as a puppy in his office. Like almost any puppy picture you have ever seen, Panda's face is the embodiment of joy, excitement, hope, and love. As with any puppy, you just get the sense that he can't wait to interact with you, play with you, and show you how much he enjoys your presence. We believe it is helpful to have a reminder of the type of behavior and attitude we hope to project to others; for Garry, that picture of Panda does the trick. Likewise, on Sharon's dresser is a picture of Pup when he won his blue ribbon. It serves to remind her that it can be done, and all you have to do is try. Pup did—and he won!

One of the ongoing tragedies of our close relationships with dogs is that they have such short lives compared to ours. Where we live sixty, seventy, or eighty years or more, they are only with us for an average of ten to fifteen years. Dogs live intense, highly engaged lives in that short time, which is one of the reasons human beings like dogs so very much—they remind us that time is limited and that how we live our lives and treat people now is important. In our research, we were fortunate to stumble across the following story, which stresses the importance of living life fully.

Thomas Neil Rodriguez is a resident of New York City who works as a deejay for a living.[2] In December 1999, he adopted Poh, an eight-week-old Lab/Pit Bull-mix puppy from the North Shore Animal League on Long Island. Thomas says that Poh grew up a "really, really strong, really healthy" dog with a great personality. Fast-forward fifteen years to January 2015, when Thomas learned that Poh was suffering from renal failure. A checkup showed that Poh had a softball-sized tumor on his liver and many other tumors in and around his kidneys. The prognosis by the veterinarian was not positive. "With those types of symptoms, the doctor can't really give you a timeline," Thomas said, noting that Poh could have had anywhere from days to years to live.[3]

Thomas and his fiancé decided to make the most of Poh's time with them and came up with the idea for a "bucket list" of things to do for and with the dog. Because Thomas's job takes him on the road a lot, he set up his work itinerary with Poh in mind and began taking the dog along and documenting their travels on Instagram.[4] Thomas observed that Poh's spirits really seemed to perk up on the road and, together with his fiancée; they visited more than thirty-five cities and drove more than 40,000 miles. Thomas reports that Poh "…[had] no problem in the car. By the end of the trip, we had figured out which supplements to give him and the right meal to give him and he loved it as far as I could tell."[5] In fact, Thomas felt that Poh enjoyed the opportunity to get out, explore, and see and smell things rather than simply lie around at home.

We agree with Thomas that there is a valuable lesson to be learned from this situation. As Thomas says, "A lot of people are ready to give up [on their dog]. I think some people might have already put their dog down at this point, but he still has these bursts of energy. If Poh has taught me anything, it's that we can't give up—we gotta live."[6]

Thomas and his fiancée did their best to see that Poh's last days were enjoyable and happy. What more could they have offered a dear best friend like Poh, and

---

2   Retrieved July 21, 2015, from http://www.nbcnewyork.com/news/local/Poh-Dogs-Big-Adventure-Dog-With-Cancer-Bucket-List-Trips-Instagram-305763901.html

3   *Ibid.*

4   Visit https://instagram.com/pohthedogsbigadventure/?hl=en to see Poh's travels on Instagram.

5   Retrieved July 21, 2015, from http://time.com/3902490/poh-labrador-road-trip/

6   *Ibid.*

what more could have Poh offered than spending his time enjoying the company of those he loves. Poh passed away in February 2016, at the age of sixteen years and four months, more than a year after his diagnosis.

Garry's friend Dr. Gary Stroud said he thinks dogs are a reflection of our better natures. By this, he means that we see the qualities we wish to consistently see in ourselves and others in the behavior of man's best friend. Our guess is that at least part of what drew you to this book was the title and the recognition that dogs do have something important to teach us. We can't begin to guess what you might do because you have read this book, but it is our hope that you will take a critical look at your life and relationships and make changes that will bring you and others more joy.

You can look at magic in one of two ways. It can be something that is unbelievable and otherworldly, like conjuring spells or riding on a flying carpet. But there is also the magic of our experiences and the exhilarating feeling of wonder we have when holding our children in our arms, walking across the stage to receive a degree, or stepping off the plane in an exotic location. As Bob Lucas suggests in his book *231 Ways to Say I Love You…and Mean It*, "Select a pet together. Go to a local adoption agency or SPCA to find an abandoned animal to become part of your family."[7] There is the magic of bringing a new dog home and watching that bundle of fur become one of your best friends in life. That is the kind of magic you can touch and feel forever.

While we hope you feel good and have enjoyed the book, and we recognize that it is nice that you now know the seven secrets of happiness as embodied by dogs, they will remain abstract principles until you begin to live them in your life—until you put these secrets into practice.

Good luck, and may you and your dog remain best friends for many years to come.

—GARRY MCDANIEL & SHARON MASSEN

---

7   Lucas, Robert W. (2016). *231 Ways to Say I Love you . . . and Mean It*, p. 67.

APPENDIX

GREAT DOG RESOURCES

As dog lovers ourselves, we have been amazed at the wealth of information on the Internet on dogs, and we can't include all of the helpful websites here. In this section, we want to share just a few that provide information you might find helpful. We are not endorsing nor do we have a financial interest or relationship with any of the sites. Rather, we are simply sharing sources of information on dog products, feed, health, and more. If you know of cool sites that you think we should know about, please email us at garrymcdaniel@aol.com or trents1940@aol.com.

LEARNING ABOUT YOU AND YOUR DOG

The following websites are a sample of those you can visit to take online self-assessments on a variety of dog- and people-related topics.

Dognition (Users are charged a fee for completing the assessment)
www.dognition.com

The Dognition assessment was developed by leading canine scientists and trainers to give you a perspective on how your dog sees the world. By understanding your dog's mind, you will build a deeper connection with the personality of your dog. Twenty fun, easy games comprise the Dognition assessment, which you can take at home. When you complete the assessment, you will receive your dog's unique profile report, which describes your dog's unique genius. The report will also provide insight into the way your dog thinks and an in-depth breakdown of the results of each game.

Dog Breed Selector
dogtime.com/quiz/dog-breed-selector

Selecting a dog is a big decision. This twenty-one item quiz will help you consider various factors that will impact what kind of dog is best for your family. These include questions about your health, home environment, children, activity level, and so on. By completing the quiz, you will get several options of dog breeds that are most suitable based on your answers.

Is My Dog Spoiled?

barkpost.com/spoiled-dog-quiz

It is normal to wonder: just how spoiled is my dog? As owners, we might treat them like human babies, make them custom food, do their nails, and sing them lullabies . . . but that's all normal, right? This short, fun quiz will give you a humorous look at how spoiled your dog is.

How Much Do You Love Dogs?

brainfall.com/quizzes/how-much-do-you-love-dogs

If you wonder if your dog is spoiled, you might also wonder just how much you love dogs. This fun quiz asks a number of questions that lead to a percentage score indicating just how much you love dogs.

INTERESTING DOG INFORMATION

DogPlay

www.dogplay.com

DogPlay provides articles, information, advice, and opinions on our relationships with our dogs. The purpose of this website and the information, articles, and items produced in association with DogPlay is to improve the welfare of the domestic canine by encouraging a higher level of interaction between people and the dogs they've chosen.

American Kennel Club

www.akc.org

The American Kennel Club (AKC) is a not-for-profit organization and the largest purebred dog registry in the world. The AKC is also the governing body for more than 22,000 dog events a year, including conformation (dog shows) and exciting sports like agility, obedience, rally, tracking, lure coursing, earthdog, and herding trials, among others. The AKC offers a comprehensive range of programs, events, and services designed to support and enrich the lives of dogs—purebreds and mixed-breeds alike—and their families.

WebMD (for dogs)

pets.webmd.com/dogs

If you have a dog, then at some point your furry friend is going to experience some sort of ailment. WebMD is a great site not only for people but also for pets, including dogs. The WebMD site for dogs provides a great deal of information on the major illnesses and diseases dogs may experience. You can also access information on nutrition, training, puppy care, preventive care, and common conditions that may affect your dog.

Huffington Post
www.huffingtonpost.com/news/dogs

The *Huffington Post* is a leading news and commentary site that provides a wide variety of information on local, regional, national, and international topics. The *Huffington Post* has a section dedicated just to dogs. On this site, you will find timely articles, commentaries, and other interesting facts on dogs.

Puppy Lover News
puppylovernews.com

The mission of *Puppy Lover News* is to promote and report on interesting stories and fascinating facts that will educate you about puppies and dogs. You will find *Puppy Lover News* as a go-to source for new and exciting stories about your canine friends.

Purina
www.purina.com/dogs

Purina is an industry-leading provider of pet food and research on the well-being of pets. The company is ranked as one of the top three places to work by Glassdoor.com and has a great pet-friendly work environment. Purina's website provides a great deal of information on dogs, including cutting-edge research, how to select the right dog for you and your family, how to pick the right dog food, and wonderful examples of people making a difference in the lives of their pets. If you go to the Purina videos on YouTube, you will see some hilarious segments on dogs. Finally, you can also learn about Purina's Better with Pets Summit, which brings together leading scientists and pet experts to showcase how innovations are enhancing relationships between people and pets.

COOL DOG ART

Artists play a very important role in society by providing depictions and representations of life through a variety of unique and creative mediums. There are many artists who devote all or a great portion of their art to dogs; the following websites represent just a handful of the many intriguing artists and galleries with works you will find interesting.

Robert McClintock
robertmcclintock.com/galleries/dog-breeds

Robert McClintock develops art using a hybrid mix of original photographs, hand manipulation, and painting using a digital technique. The results are amazing works that are unique and colorful. Many of Robert's pieces feature dogs, and the link provided here will take you to his website. We think you will be impressed with the quality and creativity of his work.

Swamp Dog and Friends
www.swampdogandfriends.com

While visiting New Orleans one year to speak at a conference, Garry happened to stumble across the Swamp Dog and Friends gallery, located in the French Quarter. The gallery is owned by Robin Bell and Jennie Alexandry and features original work and prints of very clever and entertaining dogs in unique circumstances. The website is well worth a visit.

George Rodrique
georgerodrigue.com

If you follow dog art, you are almost certainly familiar with the work of George Rodrigue. Rodrigue grew up in the heart of Cajun country and has developed a unique style to capture the essence of his experiences and ideas as they relate to Louisiana and the South. He is very popular for his "blue dog" paintings, and his renown has grown to the point where he has galleries in several major cities. Visit the website to view originals, prints, books, and other works by this great and talented artist.

Gallery Rinard
galleryrinard.com/rinard.php

Gallery Rinard is located in the heart of the French Quarter and is a whimsical showplace known for its unbridled use of color, unique custom framing, and sense of humor. Gallery founder and artist Matt Rinard and other fine New Orleans artists have created a number of offerings featuring dogs (and cats). Gallery Rinard prides itself on not intimidating people who have questions about art or the art-making process, so if you are in the French Quarter and are tired of being accosted by mimes and tarot card readers in historic Jackson Square, stop by and bask in the relative calm and visual delights of Gallery Rinard.

DOG JEWELRY AND CLOTHING

Dog lovers not only like to be out and about with their dogs, but also they like to flaunt their affections through the jewelry and clothing that they and their dogs wear. Garry has a great mug he obtained from a pottery street vendor in Columbus, Ohio with the classic saying, "I wish I were the kind of person my dog thinks I am!" Sharon has several professional photos of Pup on tables and her dresser, as well as on the wall in the office. The sites listed here are just a smattering of the excellent businesses and foundations that offer products that will tickle your fancy.

The Animal Rescue Site
www.theanimalrescuesite.com

The Animal Rescue Site provides food and vital care for some of the eight million unwanted animals given to shelters every year in the United States, as well as to animals in desperate need around the world. More than four million animals are put to death every year in the United States alone because they are abandoned. When you visit the Animal Rescue Site, you will see a huge variety of dog-related clothing, jewelry, accessories, and products for you and your home to remind you of how special our canine friends are to each of us.

In the Company of Dogs
www.inthecompanyofdogs.com

In the Company of Dogs, founded in 1994, offers gifts and gear for dogs and the people who share their lives. You'll find beds, harnesses, carriers, gates, crates, ramps, feeders, toys, dog apparel, and more. As a dog lover, express your appreciation for your best friend with dog-themed artwork, home decor, apparel, and jewelry.

14K9
14k9.com

This interesting site has a variety of gold and silver jewelry representing purebred dogs as well as pieces to commemorate show wins or titles.

Lisa Welch Designs
www.lisawelchdesigns.com/dog-themed-jewelry

Dog lovers walk in style, so why not show that style in exquisite quality every day of the week? Lisa Welch Designs features high-quality dog-themed jewelry with collars, fire hydrants, bowls, and, of course, pawprint designs; all are uniquely designed by Lisa Welch and have a satin finish combined with a high polish finish for a bold and sophisticated look crafted for comfort for animal lovers. Lisa Welch Designs offers one-of-a-kind designs, unmatched in the pet and fashion industry today, which are crafted from the highest quality of materials and craftsmanship. Very impressive jewelry and well worth your time to visit!

ACTIVITIES FOR KIDS WHO LOVE DOGS

A number of websites provide suggestions and downloads designed to provide children and dogs with hours of fun activities.

DLTK's Crafts for Kids

www.dltk-kids.com/animals/pets-dogs.htm

The DLTK website provides you with a number of craft projects for children of different ages. Crafts and downloadable projects include jigsaw puzzles, calendars, craft boxes, treat bags, dog greeting cards, door hangers, and instructions on how to draw dogs.

American Kennel Club's *The Dog Listener*

www.akc.org/pdfs/PBSAF2.pdf

Not only does the American Kennel Club's website have a wealth of information and facts about dogs, but they provide a free downloadable and printable booklet to help educate children about dog safety. The free guide includes games, mazes, puzzles, and coloring pages that encourage safe behavior around dogs and teaches children how to "read" dog behavior and respond appropriately. It is a great resource for children, parents, and educators.

Print Activities

www.printactivities.com

Click on "Animal Printables" and then "Dogs" to find downloadable activity pages for kids who love dogs. Dog activity pages include word puzzles, dog-shaped mazes, counting mazes, dot-to-dot prints, coloring pages, cryptograms, and more. These fun and educational worksheets are suitable for preschool through elementary school-aged children.

Sparky School House

sparkyschoolhouse.org

Who doesn't remember Sparky the Fire Dog? Sparky's website has a huge variety of activities, videos, and games for your child or classroom. This interactive site provides children with comics, e-cards, games, and even mobile apps that will help educate them about important safety issues.

Animal Planet

www.animalplanet.com/pets/dogs

Millions of children watch Animal Planet's great TV shows every week. Not surprisingly, the Animal Planet website offers a myriad of videos and articles on topics such as how to train your dog, different types of dogs and the jobs they perform, interviews with dog experts, and many more topics relating to our canine friends—and check out the Puppy Cam!

DOG RESEARCH

National Canine Research Council

www.nationalcanineresearchcouncil.com

The National Canine Research Council publishes reliable research to promote a better understanding of the human–dog relationship. The Council also conducts its own research on issues impacting the human–canine bond, including the dynamics of popular attitudes toward dogs and canine aggression.

Horowitz Dog Cognition Lab

dogcognition.wordpress.com

Many of you may have read Dr. Alexandra Horowitz's excellent book *Inside of a Dog: What Dogs See, Smell, and Know*. Dr. Horowitz and her team at the Horowitz Dog Cognition Lab at Barnard University study the behavior and cognition of the domestic dog by observing companion dogs in their natural environment. The team also recruits dogs and their owners to participate in fun and interesting studies. This site provides the visitor with some of the latest research findings on dogs.

Duke Canine Cognition Center, Evolutionary Anthropology Department, Duke University

evolutionaryanthropology.duke.edu/research/dogs

The Duke Canine Cognition Center is dedicated to the study of dog psychology. Its goal is to understand the flexibility and limitations of dog cognition. In the course of their research, center staff gain a window into the mind of animals and apply their knowledge of dog cognition to improving programs in which dogs are bred and trained to help humans (e.g., service dogs for the disabled). Of special interest is the fact that the center invites dog owners living in the vicinity of Duke University (Raleigh/Durham/Chapel Hill) to volunteer their pet dogs to play fun problem-solving games in which they can win food or toys.

American Kennel Club Canine Health Foundation

www.akcchf.org/research

The American Kennel Club Canine Health Foundation conducts scientific research and supports the dissemination of health information to prevent, treat, and cure canine disease. The site provides links to success stories of past research projects, information about grant and research opportunities, canine health-related resources, and news about the latest advances in canine research and health.

Zelda Wisdom

www.zeldawisdom.com

A favorite feature of this site is "Day-to-Day Dogma" from Zelda, the site's namesake Bulldog. Zelda dresses up in different costumes for each day's pearl of wisdom and is often pictured with one of her doggie pals. You can subscribe to the email list to receive a daily passage from Zelda in your inbox every day. Zelda also has a really cute collection of greeting cards for all kinds of occasions.

"So God Made a Dog"

https://www.youtube.com/watch?v=VDrabmm421I

This video will make you smile and cry, giggle and shout. It is a great tribute to the many sides of a dog and how each dog has many unique qualities that make that dog special to someone. And, for the dog, that special someone becomes his person to love, to smile at, to snuggle, and to protect; the dog's person is everything to him.

ACKNOWLEDGMENTS

Thanks go to my parents, who encouraged my interest and love of animals. I also am deeply indebted to my wife, Lauren, and my children, Ian and Julia, who always make life richer with their unfailing sense of humor and their faith that this book would come to be. Since this book is about dogs, I must also thank Spot, Domino, and Panda—three English Springer Spaniels who were our friends, playmates, protectors, and best buddies. They brought amazing joy and fulfillment to our family and served as the inspiration for this book.

I also extend my appreciation to the many individuals who provided stories that have been included in this book. Christopher Reggio, managing director at Lumina Media, and Amy Deputato, our editor, shared their wisdom and guidance to help bring the book to fruition. Chris and Amy, thanks for believing in us. Thanks to Professor Bruce Ramsey, program chair of marketing at Franklin University, for his insightful and innovative ideas about helping others understand the unique approach of the book. Most of all, we would like to thank all of you who love dogs and see our reflection in their eyes.

—Garry McDaniel, Senior Author

I, too, thank my parents; my best friend, Mark; and my other friends for encouraging the faith that I always had in the intelligence of animals. Although my earliest dog best friend, Gladys, a beautiful Collie that firmly believed she was another Lassie, and my darling Snowdie, were my constant companions for years in my young life, my other best friends were various animals, such as my hamsters, that shared a special relationship with me and my dogs . As you read this book, you will learn more about the loving, loyal, and faithful animals that have spent their lives with me and others through their own stories. Special thanks to Jagade Royal Walker—Pup for short—who spent sixteen fantastic years explaining to me that he was a person, not a dog.

—Sharon Massen, Coauthor

INDEX

AFTERWORD

In the past four decades, I have written nearly forty books and compilations of my own and have trained and spoken to thousands of professionals from around the world. Many of the sessions and classes that I have facilitated focused on the areas of interpersonal communication, diversity, supervision, management, and leadership. So, when the authors of this book asked me to provide some insights, I was flattered that they would think of me for this honor. Even so, I was initially a bit hesitant to accept their invitation because, even though I have owned dogs throughout my life, I consider myself a "cat person." I must admit that the concept of finding happiness in life by studying dog behavior seemed like a novel approach to examining a variety of important life and workplace skills. Still, as someone who has researched, written about, and taught the topics addressed in the book, I was not completely sold on the idea of using an analogy between dog behavior and that of humans. How could such comparisons really be made, and why would the authors need an entire book to make their point?

With all that said, I must admit that I was pleasantly surprised and impressed as I read through the text of *The Dog's Guide to Your Happiness*. My reluctance and skepticism proved unfounded. Because of the expertise of both authors, the subject matter has been handled competently and in a manner that will provide value for any reader. Not only did they effectively identify canine behavior, they also did a splendid job explaining how readers could translate lessons learned from dogs to create happiness and effectiveness in their own lives.

Throughout the book, you will find practical ideas and recommendations about how to apply concepts covered to improve your relationships with others in the workplace and in personal settings. The information is presented through a combination of research, humor, and shared stories from various dog owners. Each chapter contains strategies designed to give readers an appreciation of ways in which dogs can guide them to greater happiness. The book delves into the seven canine behaviors that translate to human happiness:

- Loyalty
- Communication
- Play
- Unconditional love
- Forgiveness
- Positive attitude
- Life balance

In what could be a book on typically academic and potentially boring topics, the authors have successfully taken a light-hearted and upbeat approach to presenting strategies that anyone can apply immediately to bring back more joy and happiness to their life.

I hope that you've enjoyed reading this book as much as I did. Live, love, and laugh—life is too short not to be happy! Ruff!

—Robert W. Lucas
Award-Winning Author and Performance Consultant
www.robertwlucas.com

PHOTO CREDITS

ABOUT THE AUTHORS

Garry McDaniel is an award-winning professor who teaches graduate and undergraduate courses in business management. He has written books on leadership strategy and conflict management and frequently speaks across the United States and internationally on topics such as leadership development, employee engagement, personal and organizational change, life balance, and what humans and businesses can learn from dogs to improve their lives. Garry lives with his wife, Lauren; his two children; and his English Springer Spaniel, Panda.

Sharon Massen is a professor of business writing and communication. She has written many articles as well as two books and frequently speaks on topics including business communication, office management, and what humans can learn from dogs to become better workers and managers. Sharon's family includes her husband, Mark, and children of friends all over the country who call them Aunt Sharon and Uncle Mark.